HOW YOU MAKE THE SALE

FRANK McNAIR

HOW YOU MAKE THE SALE

What every new salesperson needs to know

SOURCEBOOKS, INC.®
NAPERVILLE, ILLINOIS

This publication is designed to provide accurate and authoritative information in regard to the subject matter covered. It is sold with the understanding that the publisher is not engaged in rendering legal, accounting, or other professional service. If legal advice or other expert assistance is required, the services of a competent professional person should be sought.—*From a Declaration of Principles Jointly Adopted by a Committee of the American Bar Association and a Committee of Publishers and Associations*

Published by Sourcebooks, Inc.
P.O. Box 4410, Naperville, Illinois 60567-4410
(630) 961-3900
FAX: (630) 961-2168
www.sourcebooks.com

Library of Congress Cataloging-in-Publication Data

McNair, Frank.
How you make the sale : 8 keys to selling without fear / Frank McNair.
p. cm.
Includes index.
ISBN 1-4022-0435-3 (alk. paper)
1. Selling. I. Title: 8 keys to selling without fear. II. Title.

HF5438.25.M42 2005
658.85--dc22

2005019884

Printed and bound in the United States of America.
VP 10 9 8 7 6 5 4 3 2 1

Dedication

To the memory of Marvin Fowler—my maternal grandfather and a consummate salesman.

And for Laura, who believes in me and bought my proposal for marriage and a life together.

My life has been immeasurably enriched by life with both of these folks, and I am grateful beyond words.

Table of Contents

Acknowledgments ix
Introduction: Selling Is *Not* a Black Art xi
Chapter 1: Selling as Service 1
Chapter 2: How Buyers Decide to Buy 19
Chapter 3: How Does a Sale Unfold? 39
Chapter 4: Research Prior to the Sale: Identifying Hot Buttons and Flagging Landmines 59
Chapter 5: Meet and Greet: You Never Get a Second Chance to Make a Good First Impression 75
Chapter 6: Discovery: Questioning for Results 99
Chapter 7: Features and Benefits: The Difference and Why It Matters 137
Chapter 8: Making the Case/Presenting the Solution . . .169
Chapter 9: The Objective Is Objections: Dealing with Resistance 205
Chapter 10: Closing: It's Okay to Ask for the Order 233
Chapter 11: Following-Up for Ongoing Profitability 255
Chapter 12: Final Things—Launching Your Sales Ship for a Successful Voyage 283

Index 309
About the Author 317

Acknowledgments

I am grateful to so many people who helped me learn the fundamentals—and then the nuances—of the selling game. Marvin Fowler was my maternal grandfather, and he was a salesman *par excellence.* I am grateful for every minute spent with him, and regularly recognize things I learned by osmosis while tagging along as he did his work.

Chuck Chambers schooled me on the difference between product features and consumer benefits when I worked for him at Sara Lee, and it is a lesson he taught wonderfully well. He bears no blame for the phrasing, but he—more than anyone else—taught me "If a feature doesn't matter to the customer, it doesn't matter. Period."

Many of my colleagues at Douglas Battery Company were excellent salespeople, and I learned much from them. Charlie Johnson and Paul Labaugh were especially apt teachers. To this day I have never met anyone who could question and listen better than Charlie. I am also indebted to Tommy Douglas who let me—at the ripe old age of thirty-three—run a nationwide sales organization and play the sales game with real money.

Allen Lippman taught me how to be direct—it is a lesson I am still learning, though I'll never be as good at it as he is. I am grateful for his example, and for the opportunities he gave me to work with his clients and to listen to him as he mentored them in the fundamentals of selling.

My clients have taught me much—both by example and by exception. I am especially indebted to the sales teams at Amarr Garage Doors, The Flow Automotive Companies, Krispy Kreme Doughnut Corporation, and Oakwood Homes. These are very different product lines, but each company has some crackerjack salespeople.

I am thankful beyond words to Andrea Pedolsky of Altair Literary Agency, who believed in this book and found it a home at Sourcebooks. She is everything a good agent should be: coach, mentor, advocate, and friend.

I am particularly indebted to Peter Lynch—who sold this book to his editorial colleagues at Sourcebooks and was a pleasure to work with every step of the way. Peter's professionalism and easy manner redeemed the world of editors for me after a difficult experience with a previous editor. I wish we had met sooner, and hope for a long and profitable relationship with Peter and with Sourcebooks

To all these folks—and many others I may have missed—I offer thanks and gratitude. Each one of them helped to teach me what I know of selling and I am in their debt. They are a big part of whatever makes this book useful and helpful. I will, however, have to own any mistakes and omissions myself.

Have fun reading this book, and happy selling!

Introduction: Selling Is *Not* a Black Art

So you think you want to sell? Perhaps you've already tasted a measure of success in sales—you know you have at least some aptitude for this discipline, and you like what you've tasted. You like listening to customers, you like building relationships with them, and you like helping them select a product or service that meets their needs and solves their problems. You think—in time—you could be *really good* at this selling business. But you still have a couple of reservations...

Or maybe you are new to the sales game—you don't normally do sales work, but have been given an assignment that requires you to get out there and sell. You are not altogether sure the sales life is for you, and many of the sales people you have known in your life have reinforced—or even exacerbated—your reservations:

- Your first reservation has to do with worldview. You've often heard salespeople say things like "I really slam-dunked that one," or, "I knocked him in the creek!" as they talk about interactions with their customers. But you really don't see sales as a competition, one where the customer has to lose for the salesperson to win. And you think to yourself, "There must be a better way!"

- Your second concern is harder to articulate, but just as important. It goes something like this: "They make selling sound so *hard*—so many tricks and maneuvers, so many moves and counter moves. It winds up sounding like electrical engineering married to guerrilla warfare." *Does it really have to be that way?*
- Your third concern is one of style—both personal and sartorial. Do I have to dress like the car salesmen I see on television—plaid jacket, beltless slacks, plastic shoes? And do I have to wave my arms and gesture wildly while screaming, "Come on down, we're dealin'!" at the top of my lungs? *I'm just not sure that is me. Or that I ever want it to be me!*
- Your final concern is one of *aptitude*—some people are just *born* to be salespeople. And you are not so sure that you're one of them—you don't have the "gift of gab" that many folks seem to think is required of good salespeople. You wonder: *Can a person of good intentions and reasonable intelligence learn to sell? If they are not naturally glib?*

If you've ever had any of these thoughts—or any of dozens of other reservations about selling—then this is the book for you. I titled this book *How You Make the Sale* because I believe you can sell the product that interests you to people you value while still maintaining your integrity, your sense of self, and your current wardrobe and personality. And—while selling is difficult—it requires no superhuman aptitude. Selling is a learnable skill, and I can help you learn it.

Selling is not a black art. You do not have to sacrifice a live chicken at the full moon to the god of sales quotas to make a good living as an ethical, principled salesperson. You simply have to listen, process what you hear, and match your product or service to the problem that brought the customer into the market in the first place.

You do not have to change your worldview to sell successfully. In fact, the more ethical and customer-focused you are, the more successful you will be in the long term. Sales people who value their customers and treat them with respect gain their trust and generate repeat business. And repeat sales to satisfied customers are the most profitable sales of all.

While learning the nuances of selling can be difficult, selling is not a science—rocket or otherwise. You do not have to master arcane terms and complicated flowcharts to sell your customers the products they need to meet their needs and solve their problems.

Selling is a *process*—a rather simple process, really—that moves logically from beginning to end in a series of eight predictable, easily identifiable steps. The steps are simply building blocks—each step builds upon the previous one as the salesperson and the prospective customer move together from their first interaction until the final sale.

Every step in the sales process requires a particular skill set, that's true. But there's no need to panic just yet—all the skills are learnable skills, and you already use many of the skills in your day-to-day living. Anyway, what in life doesn't require skills? Using a phone, driving a car, reading a book, relating to our friends, family, and colleagues—each of these requires a unique skill set as well. And we have all managed to master these skills.

Selling can be learned, and this book will help you learn it. This book will teach you how to name each step in the sales process and how to recognize where you are as you move from step to step. You will also learn how to use skills you already have to aid you in hearing your prospective customer and tailoring with him or her the solution that meets their needs or solves the problem that brought them to you in the first place.

A quick word about what this book is not. This book is not a treatise on how to trick folks into buying from you. This is not a book of scam tricks or high-pressure sales tactics that force the buyer to make a choice he or she might not yet be ready to make. Sorry. If that's the book you want, you need to slip this one back on the shelf. That's not the kind of selling I believe in, the kind of selling I like, nor the kind of selling I do. It's certainly not the kind of selling I teach! So I can't help you.

But if you want to learn to sell professionally, then this is the book for you. If you are willing to work, try new things, step out of old ways of being, and occasionally work without a net, then this is the book for you. Finally, if you are excited about the prospect of meeting people who have a problem and hatching out a solution that fits you both, then this is the book for you.

You *can* sell it, and I'm going to show you how. Let's get to work!

1
Selling as *Service*

Most people have a mental image of salespeople talking customers into buying. In fact, there is some (far too much, actually) of that in the world. That's not what we—you and I—are going to be about. Because it's not who we—you, me, you and me—are.

(A note about how this book is written: I use the collective pronoun "we" here by choice, not by accident. I am not going to be off in the distance telling you what you should do. I am not some detached, omniscient onlooker. I am a sales *practitioner*—I sell, too. All the time. It's how I make my living. And you and I (that's *we* too) are going to walk together down the path to the sale. We are going to reflect on our own experiences when we have been consumers. We are going to think about what works and what doesn't when we are buying. And we are going to sell from a service mindset. And that's going to make all the difference—for us, and especially for our customers.)

Let's look together at two different sales perspectives. You can see which one feels the most comfortable for you.

Combatant Selling vs. Service Selling

Though there are hundreds of sales models in the world, they can be sorted into one of two distinct groups based on how the sales person sees the customer. The more common (and more stereotypical) of the two models sees the customer as a combatant—someone with whom we are doing battle. The language in this model sounds much like the language of modern warfare. You'll hear salespeople talk of their *strategy* and their *tactics*, discussions of *outflanking* the customer, and measures for *attacking* weaknesses, *countering* resistance, and even *defeating* objections. You'll even hear conversations about guerrilla marketing—as if you were going out in camouflage and face paint to sneak a sale past an unwitting sentry.

I once did a great deal of consulting work for a company of this sort. These folks—many of them anyway—viewed the customer as the enemy, and I could never fully move them away from this view. "All buyers are liars," they said to themselves. And then they charged straight ahead based on that assumption, telling lies themselves in pursuit of the sale. It was not a pretty picture...

The combatant view of selling marks the customer as the "enemy." We "win" by defeating the customer in the sales interaction. In fact, we "win" when we make the sale—which means that the customer "loses" when he or she buys from us. Is this some kind of perverse and twisted logic or what? How can we—in good conscience—make a sale when we know that the customer is losing by buying from us?

We can't. We can't stay in business for the long term (and generate repeat or referral customers) by making sales where the buyer loses. And repeat/referral sales are the most profitable of all sales. So we (that's you and me, Bub) are going to focus on win-win selling—selling where we serve the customer by helping him or her make the best possible choice to solve the problem that took him or her into the market in the first place.

I'm talking here about selling as *service*—that is, service to the customer. We are talking about a sales model—and a mind set—where the salesperson adds value by what he knows, what she can teach, and how he or she structures a sale to meet the customer's needs and solve the customer's problems.

Doesn't that sound like a better, more appealing career for you—a better way to live your professional life? We see our customers as, among other things, colleagues. And we walk with them toward the solution that is best for them and for us—a solution that meets their needs and solves their problems while helping us make an honest living.

Your role as a salesperson is to *serve*—to serve the customer, to serve the demands of the sales process, and to serve your own needs for significance and competence by being the very best salesperson you can be. This shift to a service mindset is an important and profound transformation. And it transforms not only your self-understanding, but also the buying experience for the customer, the customer's long-term satisfaction with you and your products, and your success as a salesperson.

> *The customer is not your enemy. You don't win if the customer loses. Together, the two of you are walking toward a solution that addresses the customer's problem and puts a living wage in your pocket. You are colleagues, not competitors—never forget this essential fact.*

Let's take a quick look at the difference between products that are *bought* and products that are *sold*. We'll also reflect some about comparisons between products sold directly to end users, and business-to-business sales.

More Products Are Bought Than Are Sold

The marketplace holds tens of thousands of products from which we choose every day. And more of those products are bought than are sold, with good reason.

What does it mean when I say "more products are bought than are sold"? Just this: no one ever comes to your door selling chewing gum, do they? Or toilet tissue? Or any of the myriad other products in the grocery store. Grocery store goods, at least in general, are *bought* not *sold*. As are drugstore health and beauty aids, and most clothing and other products found in the typical suburban mall. These products are surely purchased—people go home with them every day. But they are *bought* by the consumer, not *sold* by a salesperson.

No salesperson ever calls you extolling the virtues of Crest toothpaste over those of Colgate. No one canvases your neighborhood, trying to get you to switch from Ajax scouring powder to Comet. No one calls in the middle of suppertime trying to get you to switch from Glass-Plus to Windex. Have you ever wondered why this doesn't happen? These are all well-known products; why don't they employ these types of direct-to-consumer selling?

The answer is twofold: 1) sales price and 2) dollar margin. No one canvases your neighborhood selling the average cleanser or toothpaste or window cleaner because the dollar value of the sale is too low, and the margin on the sale is not enough to support a sales force devoted solely to one-on-one sales of the product.

The products we are talking about are marketed for sure. Television ads, coupons in the newspaper, and perhaps even sampling in the store itself help to move the product from the manufacturer to the end user. But the products are not sold, per se. At least not to end users like you and me. No one could make a living selling these products—there's not enough price and not enough margin to support a salesperson going house-to-house with these products.

Put another way—as we think about service—there is not enough price or margin to support the *services* of a professional salesperson for end users. And because the products are relatively inexpensive and simple to use (and because the risk of a purchasing mistake is low) customers don't demand the services of a salesperson when making their choices. Of course—and good for salespeople like you and me—not all products fit into the serviceless category.

What Type of Products Require a Professional Salesperson?

Let's think about some of the products we use every day that *are* sold—a real salesperson touches a real customer leading to a purchase that (at least ideally) solves the customer's problems and helps the salesperson make a living wage. Or—in the case of business-to-business selling—a real person calls on a real manager and advocates that the manager buy from the salesperson to solve a problem in the company the manager represents. What products fit this description?

Well, cars for one. And houses. Boats. Motorcycles, ATVs, and personal watercraft. Most life insurance, financial instruments, and investments. Also major home appliances, most big-ticket home repairs, and high-end home-entertainment systems. Tailor-made clothing is another example, as well as high-end off-the-rack clothing. Jewelry is also an example—and the more expensive it is, the more service and consultation is required and expected. (Who wants to make a mistake on a $5,000 chunk of carbon?)

In the business-to-business arena, the universe of products *sold* rather than *bought* is enormous. Interestingly, the larger the "customer" company, the fewer products it has to *buy*. Large companies pop up on everyone's prospect radar, so salespeople are always seeking these companies out to *sell* them something. Copiers, computers, vehicles, and software are all products that merit a sales effort and can be very profitable. But even very low margin, commodity products (sugar, salt, gasoline, et al.) can be profitable when sold in volume to large corporations.

In the consumer market, other examples of things that are sold, not bought, include new jobs/careers (what are executive recruiters but salespeople?—selling on both sides of the interaction) and the selection of a college or university (now *that* is an expensive purchase!). In fact, more and more traditionally non-sales jobs (college admissions, telephone customer service jobs, even bank tellers) now contain a significant component of selling among their key responsibilities. It's not too much of a stretch to say that—in one way or another—almost everyone in the world of business is "in sales" in one way or another. Even teachers have to sell their ideas and new subject matter to the students they work with every day.

All of these are occasions where the product is truly *sold*—a salesperson adds value and provides a service that helps the buyer make the right buying decision. Beyond the fact that these purchases require a salesperson, what else do they have in common? What factors might predict that a sale will require—or at least be helped by—a salesperson? The factors for each of these sales include:

- they have a relatively high dollar value (especially versus toothpaste or scouring powder),
- they occur relatively infrequently (we buy toothpaste monthly, but a house only every seven to ten years),
- many of the decisions are moderately complex—with lots of considerations before the optimum choice is made,
- for most of these products, service and repair after the sale is a major consideration in the customer's satisfaction with the product, and
- the cost (monetary) and inconvenience (lost time; increased hassle) of a bad decision is high.

These are all areas in which a salesperson can add value for the customer, justifying the added expense of a dedicated, professional sales team.

Adding Value with Service

How do salespeople add value? What is it they do that provides a service to the customer, and justifies the expense to the company of paying the salesperson, training the salesperson, and providing benefits, expenses, and the other perks that keep the sales force in the field?

We could make this complicated, but let's not. *Here are the ways you can add value as a professional salesperson*:

1) *Listen carefully to the customer* to fully discern the customer's wants and needs.

2) *Clarify the customer's wants and needs* both for yourself and (often) for the customer himself. It always amazes me how much the customer learns as we walk towards the purchase together. Clarifying the customer's needs is one service a professional salesperson provides to add value for his or her customers.
3) *Determine the problem the customer is trying to solve*, so that you (the salesperson) can solve the problem in the most appropriate manner.
4) *Know your own (and your competitor's) product lines* so completely that you can select—from among all the reasonable options—the product or service that best meets the customer's needs and solves the customer's problems.
5) *Present the solution so the customer sees and appreciates the benefits* of the solution, and understands why this solution is the best one for his situation.
6) *Help the customer complete the transaction* in other ways: creative financing, advocating for the customer with management, arranging delivery, and so forth, and
7) *Follow-up after the sale* to ensure that the customer is satisfied with his or her purchase, and to make any additional sales that would add additional value to the customer.

In each case, the salesperson's primary job is *serving* the customer—doing whatever is necessary to help the customer meet his needs, solve his problems, and leave happy.

There are so many myths about selling—we'd never have

time to dispel them all, even if this book was twice as long as it is, and was devoted solely to dispelling myths. That said, some myths as are so pervasive—and so pernicious—that we need to deal with them right out of the gate. Let's take a look at three key myths that can derail a sales career. These myths include:

1. Sales is all about *making the sale*,
2. You have to "control" the customer to make the sale, and
3. Customers "buy" your company, not you.

It Ain't about the Sale

In many sales systems, the focus is on making the sale. I *do not* embrace that view. It is too narrow to do the sales process—or the customer—justice.

I believe the sale is a by-product of providing excellent service to the customer, solving the problems that the customer brings to the interaction, and asking for the business. If you can solve the problems (solve them better, more economically, more quickly, and more thoroughly) than the other salespeople chasing the sale, you will make the sale.

This is an important point. Focusing on the sale before you have fully understood the customer's needs and wants and problems is getting things all out of order. Imagine if you rushed up to someone you have just met (someone whom you find attractive) and saying, "Hi, you're really cute. Want to get married? Now?" That question may someday be the right question to pose to this person. But rushing to the proposal before you have had a chance to fully understand the other person's relationship needs, wants—and before your fully understand their perceptions of long-term relationships—will only end in disaster.

In selling, as in dating, if you take time to fully understand the customer's wants and needs and problems—you will have a better chance of filling the needs and solving the problems. And a much better chance of winding up with a customer for life! The sales steps in this book provide a systematic and logical process that will walk you from the meet and greet stage of a sales interaction all the way to presenting a solution to the customer's problem and asking for the order. The steps will also help you know how to follow-up after the sale to keep your customers satisfied so you will generate repeat sales and referral business.

The Control Problem

I believe there has been more ink spilled—and more words written—about control than the topic will ever merit. We are cautioned not to lose control of the sale, to stay in control, to never give up control. I don't really know what all this means—why all this focus on control? I think it might speak more to the neuroses of sales trainers and writers than to any eternal truth about selling.

An undue focus on control telegraphs a disturbing

underlying belief: If the salesperson does not manipulate the customer by maintaining tight control over him or her, the sale will not happen. This makes the customer an opponent—or an enemy—once again, and that is a worldview we do not want to embrace.

I still believe that if we treat our customers as colleagues we will help them discover the solution that solves their problem and, more often than not, also makes our sale. We won't get all the business, but we shouldn't get all the business. We don't have the product to solve every customer's problem, every time.

It's all about trusting the process. I trust the process. It has worked for me in my life. It can work for you, too. And it will also allow you to tell the world—with justifiable pride—"I am a service-focused salesperson who treats my customers like colleagues!"

All this nonsense about control assumes that the customer is our enemy. The customer is not the enemy. You don't win if the customer loses.

People Buy from People, Not from Companies

People buy from people—it's as simple as that. This is not to deny that companies have a history. More than once I have benefited from the fact that "we've done business with your company for years." I've also suffered from the flip side of that phrase: "we've never really worked with your company; our founder always preferred your competitor." In general, though, honest customers and buyers make rational economic choices based on the facts as they understand them. If you can educate customers about the facts (one of the services you provide as a professional salesperson) you have an excellent chance of making the sale.

Think about your own purchase behavior. When you get ready to buy a car, do you just waltz into the nearest dealership? You decide the make you are interested in (let's say it is Nissan), then ask your friends if they know anyone at the dealership. Similarly when it's time to buy a house, do you just take any old "agent on duty" when you walk into an open house? Or do you ask friends for referrals, then contract with a buyer's agent before the process even begins?

People like to do business with folks they know and trust. If they don't know or trust anyone in a particular business, they seek referrals. (I'd rather work with someone my friend knows and trusts than take blind luck in a listing of agents/salespeople!)

What keeps customers coming back—and generates the bulk of the world's referral business—is the service mindset we have talked about embracing. If you ask yourself—in every interaction with your customers—"How can I serve this customer best in this situation?" you will rarely go wrong. And you will never fall prey to "talking them into buying."

Serve your customers well. They win. You win. And everyone leaves happy.

The key to success in the whole sales game is not mastery of hard-driving sales tactics. Nor is it some magic way to trick 'em into buying. Nope, the key to the selling is learning how to: 1) listen carefully, so you can 2) craft a solution that solves the customer's problem and serves his or her needs and then, 3) ask for the order. If you can master these three concepts, you can be a successful professional salesperson. And this book will teach you these three skills.

Getting Down to Cases: A Quick Content Review

1. What is combatant selling? What are some of the characteristics of combatant selling?________________

   ____

2. What is service selling? What services does a servant salesperson offer to the customer?________________

   ____

3. What does it mean when we read "more products are bought than sold"? What are the five factors (they are listed in the chapter) that make a product one that can profitably be *sold*?________________________

   ____

   ____

4. What are the three myths that often get in the way of selling well?______________________________

____

5. What is the single most important thing you learned in this chapter? How will you discipline yourself to remember it as you move through the balance of the book?__________________________________

____

____

Making It Real: Applying What You've Learned to the Product You Sell

It's not enough to read about this service ethic—I'm less interested in what you *know* than in what you *do*. So let's do a quick review of the products, programs, or services you plan to sell as you make your career as a professional salesperson. Answer each of the questions below to help you dig deep into the ways you can serve your customer.

What is the product, program, or service you are selling?

____

____

What are the top three most common questions people have when they consider purchasing your product, program, or service?

1. ____________________________________
2. ____________________________________
3. ____________________________________

What are the primary risks if a customer makes a buying mistake with the product, program, or service that you provide? (list three)

1. ____________________________________
2. ____________________________________
3. ____________________________________

How often (in a five-year period) does the average customer make the purchase you will help him or her with?

____

____

How many dollars are at stake if a customer makes a mistake buying the product you sell? ____________________

How can you provide a service to the customer and add value to the sale by answering the customer's questions, minimizing the customer's risk, and keeping him or her informed about new developments in your product category?

Have you ever been waited on by a salesperson who was trying to control you? How did you react to that sales interaction? ____________________

How have you been taught to view the customer in other sales training you have had? Can you make the shift to seeing the customer as someone to serve, as a colleague, as a fellow-traveler on the path to a mutually beneficial solution? ____________________

Key Reminders

- Sales *is* service—and the more faithfully you serve, the more fruitfully you will sell.

- The customer is not your enemy.

- You don't win if the customer loses.

- More stuff is bought than is sold. Be someone who makes the sale happen.

- People buy from people; companies do not buy from companies.

- Service is key to the sale. We add value as salespeople when we:
    1. Listen carefully to the customer.
    2. Clarify the customer's wants and needs.
    3. Determine the problem the customer is trying to solve.
    4. Know your own (and your competitor's) product lines.
    5. Present the solution in such a way that the customer sees and appreciates the benefits.
    6. Help the customer complete the transaction.
    7. Follow-up after the sale.
    8. Quit worrying about control and serve the customer.

2
How Buyers Decide to Buy

Consumer behavior is a fascinating subject—there are entire libraries devoted to it in graduate business schools throughout the country. Fortunately for us, it is not necessary to know what is in all of those libraries to understand the basics of consumer behavior. The basics of consumer behavior and the buying decision can be summed-up in six words—none of them longer than two syllables:

> *People buy to solve a problem.*

A problem of some sort (perceived or actual) sends every prospective buyer into the market, every time. No exceptions. And the salesperson who presents the "best" (remember: the customer always defines best!) solution to the problem gets the sale. Every time. No exceptions.

So, if people buy to solve a problem, then what constitutes a problem? Interestingly, a problem is anything the customer considers a problem. The problem can be so enormous that it is apparent to the most casual observer.

Or it can be so tiny that—even after it is explained to you in great detail by the customer—you still can't understand what they are concerned about. Either way, if the customer thinks there is a problem, then there is a problem. Our job as professionals is to understand the problem precisely, solve it completely, and make the sale.

Real Problems—What They Look Like

Consider for a moment someone whose stove is on fire. In my mind that is a *real* problem. Let this issue go unattended for another five minutes and there is a *catastrophic* problem: the entire house burns down! If you were a door-to-door fire extinguisher salesperson, you'd surely find a willing buyer at this house. The customer *has* a problem. Offer fire extinguishers at a reasonable price—or at most *any* price at all—and you are in business. Problem solved, sale made, service provided, house saved, customer happy, check cashed. Ah! It's a happy world when a sale goes this smoothly!

Real problems are usually easy to identify—there's not much question about the problem the customer is trying to solve, or the need that must be met. People whose car won't run need either: 1) a repair, or 2) a different vehicle. People whose family is growing need more square footage in their house and more furniture—especially nursery furniture if the growth is from a new baby. People who have jobs where appearance is important need appropriate clothing to enhance their professional image. All of these are *real* problems, and real problems are generally easy to identify and solve. We simply ask questions, listen carefully, and match our product to the needs of the customer or prospect. Then we ask for the order, deal with objections, and close the sale. We are in business!

Real Problems with Image Issues

However, not all real problems are real problems. For example, a customer may need transportation, and that need is real enough. But a customer who needs transportation and buys a Corvette or a Porsche is meeting more than a need for transportation. Porsches and Corvettes are not primarily about transportation. They are primarily about something else—image, or the adrenaline rush of slamming through the gears at a hundred and thirty miles an hour. These cars *do* move you from one place to another. But they are not *mostly* about transportation.

Similarly, a customer may *need* a satchel in which to carry small toiletries and other items—a handbag in other words. But if the customer meets this need with a Gucci or Prada bag, then the purchase is about more than just acquiring a utilitarian bag. The product selection is about function, but it's also about statement, image, self-concept, and one's public face to the world. It's a perceived need for all these attributes—not simply a need for a container with a shoulder strap—that drives the purchase of all high-end, prestige consumer goods. Perceived needs drive more purchases than you think, and are often linked to the purchase choice in many cases where a *real* need is also present.

Here's an example. In the world of marketing, researchers often speak of "shirt sleeve" products—that is, products that consumers use in plain view of others. These are products where image can be as important as function, because consumers believe (rightly in many cases) that their peers judge them on the basis of the products they select and consume. As a consequence, many people who scrimp on underwear (because no one sees it) will insist on name brand, logo-covered outer clothing. People who use store-brand ingredients in their cooking (no one sees them) insist on serving expensive imported beer (because the label is in plain view).

This is neither good nor bad, it just *is*. And if we are going to do an effective job as professional salespeople, we have to be on the lookout for image needs every bit as hard as we watch for more concrete and apparent real needs. Real needs are usually easier to uncover, because buyers will tell you the truth about their real needs. They are less likely to own up to their needs for prestige and status—we have to intuit these needs through careful observation and judicious reading between the lines.

Perceived Problems—A Different Animal

Now let's consider another customer situation that will give a little insight into the world of *perceived* problems. To avoid besmirching anyone, I'll illustrate this example with a story from one of my wife's favorite ridiculous consumers —*me*!

I *really* like tools. In fact, it might be fair to say that I *love* tools. I am also fairly adept at using tools—I added a deck to my current house, and have done a number of other Tim-the-Tool-Man projects through the years. Still, like many aficionados of one sort or the other (think golfers, cooks, photographers, tennis players, and so forth), my tools are *far* superior to my skills.

At any rate, I have a cordless drill that I really like and have used extensively. It is my second cordless drill—a DeWalt, contractor-grade, twelve-volt, heavy-duty, bright yellow, cordless drill with a carrying case, a charger, and two battery packs. It's perfect for my needs. Except for a couple of tiny little things…

(Let me stop here and give you additional background —things you would surely uncover if you were waiting on me and trying to solve my problem by *listening closely, questioning carefully, and helping me select the perfect cordless drill* for my home improvement projects. Here are some of the things you would uncover:

1) My *drill gets relatively light use* in general—with the deck project being a notable exception,

2) I *rarely use the drill long enough in one stretch to need the reserve battery pack,*
3) Except for one time when I was trying to drill a hole in a brick wall, *twelve volts has provided more than enough power* and torque for all of my projects.)

So what's the problem? I have a high-quality tool that meets ninety-nine percent of my needs and should serve me for years to come. Any rational person can see that. Even *I* can see that! But there is a problem, and that is where the concept of "perceived problems" comes to the fore.

At the time I got my drill, twelve volts was at the high end of the range for available power in cordless tools. Some 14.4-volt tools were on the market, but twelve volts was quite enough for my needs.

But things *do* change—I regularly see 18-volt and even 24-volt cordless tools in the circulars from the big box home centers. My little drill—however good it is—seems dinky and under-powered to me now. And *that's* my problem—at least as I perceive it!

Do I need a new drill? Not really. Will my current drill serve my purposes? Probably. Do I have a rational problem? Nope. Am I going to buy a new drill in the next twelve months? More than likely…Because now my current drill seems dinky and under-powered!

I might try to rationalize this purchase to make it look like a decision based solely on the facts. One of my battery packs has failed, so I no longer have the luxury of swapping out the batteries and continuing to work—I now have to wait for the lone good battery to recharge. Of course, I've already admitted that I seldom do projects of the magnitude that requires two batteries. But I might still be able to use this rationale when I try to sell the idea of a new drill to my wife.

My drill *does* work—it actually works fine. But it seems dinky and under-powered every time I use it. So I will eventually buy a new drill. It may be after my current drill dies completely, in which case I'd be buying to solve a *real* problem, just like the homeowner with the kitchen fire. But more than likely, I'll buy a drill before the current one quits. I'll be solving my *perceived* problem—that the drill I have is dinky and under-powered.

Your customers—no matter whether they are individuals or representatives of large corporations—are always *buying to solve a problem*. The problem may be real, it may be perceived, or it may be a mix of the two. But customers always buy to solve a problem. Let's take a look now at the salesperson's (that's me and you!) role in the customer's buying process.

The Salesperson's Role in the Buying Process

Customers buy to solve problems. Sometimes the problems are real and immediately apparent; sometimes they are perceived and hard for us to fully wrap our minds around. And oftentimes they are a combination—part real problem, part perceived problem. Real, perceived, or mixed—the salesperson who offers the best solution to the problem gets the sale.

Our job as salespeople is to understand the customer's problem and, perhaps, to help them understand the problem better—to clarify it with (and for) them. Then we walk with the customer through the process of identifying possible solutions, evaluating the options, and selecting the option that best meets their purchase criteria.

The Path to Purchase

It is possible to map the stages consumers go through as they make a buying decision—there is a predictable way in which people move down the path to a purchase. The process looks like this:

The Path to Purchase

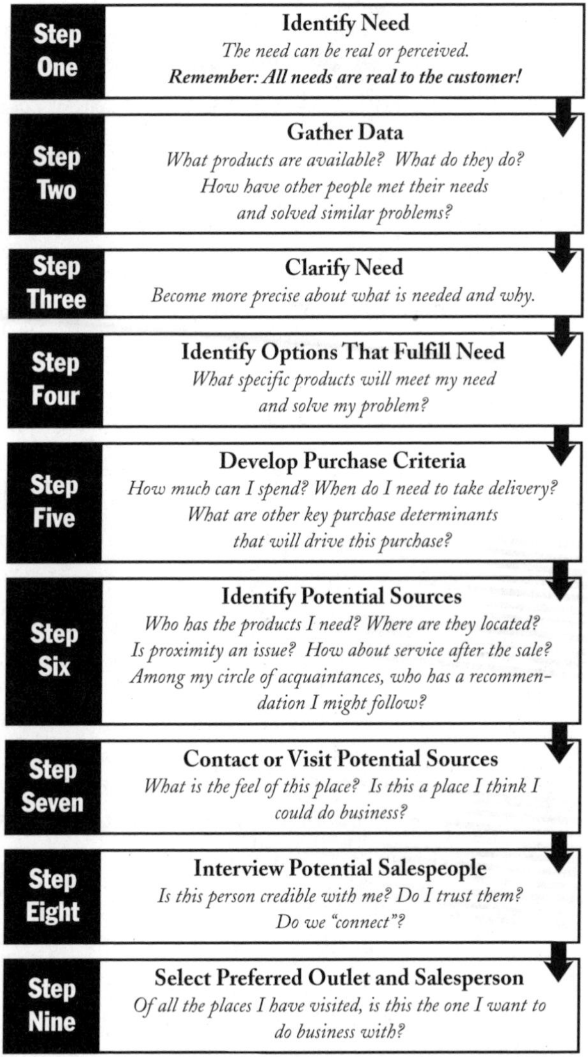

Step One	**Identify Need** *The need can be real or perceived.* ***Remember: All needs are real to the customer!***
Step Two	**Gather Data** *What products are available? What do they do? How have other people met their needs and solved similar problems?*
Step Three	**Clarify Need** *Become more precise about what is needed and why.*
Step Four	**Identify Options That Fulfill Need** *What specific products will meet my need and solve my problem?*
Step Five	**Develop Purchase Criteria** *How much can I spend? When do I need to take delivery? What are other key purchase determinants that will drive this purchase?*
Step Six	**Identify Potential Sources** *Who has the products I need? Where are they located? Is proximity an issue? How about service after the sale? Among my circle of acquaintances, who has a recommendation I might follow?*
Step Seven	**Contact or Visit Potential Sources** *What is the feel of this place? Is this a place I think I could do business?*
Step Eight	**Interview Potential Salespeople** *Is this person credible with me? Do I trust them? Do we "connect"?*
Step Nine	**Select Preferred Outlet and Salesperson** *Of all the places I have visited, is this the one I want to do business with?*

Figure 2.1

How the Path to Purchase Works

The Path to Purchase walks us logically through the process that consumers use to decide which products or services will meet their needs and solve their problems. Customers generally move through a series of steps that begins with recognizing a problem that needs a solution. They then move through a step-wise process that takes them from initial problem recognition all the way through to the final purchase.

Let's look at each of the steps in the Path to Purchase in a little more detail.

Step 1: Identify Need/Problem

In Step 1, the *prospective customer realizes that he or she has a problem*. The problem can be real or perceived, and often includes an unarticulated image component as well. Remember: people buy to solve a problem. Our first job when we meet a prospective customer is to uncover the problem he or she is trying to solve.

Step 2: Gather Data

Once a consumer can name the problem, Step 2 is to *move out into the marketplace and gather data*. What products are available to meet this need I have identified?

As an example, consider the new homeowner whose house needs painting. Identifying the symptoms of the problem (paint is cracking and peeling) is easy. Then comes the agonizing process of gathering data about paint: latex or enamel, flat, semi-gloss, or high-gloss, what manufacturer and what warranty period? And on and on and on. Most of the time you meet prospective customers when they reach Step 7 (Visit Potential Sources) of the Consumer Buying Model, but it is not uncommon for them to appear during Step 2 (Data Gathering).

Step 3: Clarify Need

As the prospective customer gathers data, he or she gradually begins to clarify the problem to be solved. To further use our paint-the-house example, let's assume the homeowner will be painting the house himself. As he learns more about paint, he can clarify his needs: he needs a latex paint (for easy clean-up) with high resistance to mildew (since he lives in a high humidity area). And he needs a paint that can withstand the extremes of temperature often served up in his area. He also needs a paint that offers good coverage—he wants to change the color of his home, and wants to do it in one coat. And he needs paint with at least a ten-year warranty, because he doesn't want to spend every other summer painting his house!

See how the need has been clarified? From a simple "I need paint," we have now developed a long list of attributes the paint needs to have if it is to solve our buyer's problem.

Step 4: Identify Options That Fulfill Need

The customer is learning as he goes—his task now is to find out what paints offer the features he seeks. He may talk to friends who have painted their houses recently, or consult publications like *Consumer Reports* or *Consumers Digest*. He is beginning to narrow the range of reasonable choices. He is discovering what options will fill his needs and solve his problems.

Step 5: Develop Purchase Criteria

The purchase criteria a customer develops are related to all the products that fit into *the range of reasonable choices*. That is, these criteria are used to sort from a universe of products —any one of which could solve the customer's problem. Purchase criteria in our example could include the following: price, availability, ability to be custom-tinted (to match existing gutters or storm doors, for instance), and a host of others.

Step 4 (Identify Options that Fulfill Need) creates a long list of possible solutions to the problem. Step 5 (Develop Purchase Criteria) allows the purchaser to eliminate from the list of possible solutions all those that cost too much or take too long or—for whatever other reason—fail to meet one or more of the buyer's purchase criteria.

Step 6: Identify Potential Sources

Here the customer runs through a series of simple—but critical—questions: Who carries the products that are in my range of reasonable choices (and that meet my purchase criteria)? Where are they located? Is proximity an issue? Among my circle of acquaintances, who has a recommendation that I might follow?

Step 7: Visit Potential Sources

Another series of questions: What is the feel of the place when I walk in the door? Is this an establishment with which I could do business? Does it appear to be a going concern? Is there anyone else in the place? How are they being treated? How are customers who telephone the business being treated?

Step 8: Identify Potential Salespeople

More questions for the consumer to wrestle with occur when they start meeting salespeople: Is this person credible with me? Does she know what she is talking about? Does he seem to listen when I speak, or am I getting a canned spiel he uses on every customer? Do I trust this person? Do I like this person? Do we "connect"? Is this someone I want to do business with?

Step 9: Select Preferred Outlet and Salesperson

One final question—the one for which the customer has been preparing throughout the whole Consumer Buying Process: Of all the places I have visited, which product, which outlet, and which salesperson seem best able to help me solve my problem?

Exceptions to the Path

The outline above is the most-common purchase model. Yet sometimes the steps happen in a slightly different order from the one presented above.

As an example, assume you are a cave-dweller in the time long before recorded history. You walk everywhere you go—walking is all you have ever known. One day you are making your way across the plain and you encounter someone riding on a horse, for heaven's sake! Your feet are tired; you look longingly at the horseback rider. You have got to have a horse!

In this case, Step 2 (Data-Gathering) preceded Step 1 (Identifying a Need). Until new data helped you realized it was possible to ride, you had no problem. You didn't even know riding was a possibility. Now that you know riding is an option (through data gathering by observing someone else on a horse), you have got a real problem (no horse).

Another example—especially with a highly rational customer—might follow this scenario. Someone realizes that she will soon be taking a lengthy automobile trip (half-way across the United States, let's say), and she has concerns about the reliability of her current vehicle. She is already at Step 1—she has identified a need. Let's say she is also someone who is very plugged-in to the state of her income and her financial life—she knows she can spend $10,000 cash (plus the trade-in value of her old vehicle) and that is all she is willing to spend.

Our sample customer has just jumped from Step 1 to Step 5. She is now looking for a new vehicle (either brand-new or new to her) that solves her problem (her undependable car). The new vehicle also must meet at least some of her other purchase criteria (able to safely make a 3,500 cross-country round-trip, comfortable on long drives, costs less than trade-in plus $10,000, and whatever else matters to her.)

The steps don't always happen in exactly the order presented in Figure 2-1, but the Path to Purchase gives us a useful starting point to examine how consumers decide to buy. And—regardless of the order in which they answer the questions—consumers must eventually answer the questions posed by the model as they move toward their purchase decision.

Getting Down to Cases: A Quick Content Review

1. Customers buy to solve a ______________________.

2. Customer problems are of (at least) two types. These types are:
   1. ______________________________
   2. ______________________________

3. What is the salesperson's role in the buying process?

   ____

   ____

4. The "Path to Purchase" lays out the steps that get taken on the way to a purchase. Who takes the steps—the salesperson or the customer? ____________

   ____

5. At what point on the Path to Purchase does the customer meet a live salesperson? ______________________

____

____

6. What is the customer doing in the steps leading up to meeting a salesperson? ______________________

____

____

Making It Real: Applying What You've Learned to the Product You Sell

Okay—it's money time. You don't get good at riding a bike by reading a book about riding a bike. You get good at riding a bike by climbing on it and pedaling like crazy while a friend holds onto the seat and swears to never let go. They *do* eventually let go—but by then you are having so much fun you forget to be mad at them.

It's the same with selling. *Reading about selling will not make you a good salesperson.* You have to work with the raw material of your life and your sales world to make any practical sense of the things we have been talking about.

Reflect on the product, program, or service you sell. Then answer these questions about the process your customers go through as they decide to buy your product from you.

Does your product address primarily *real* problems? What are the real problems consumers seek to address when they buy your product? (List as many as you can think of!)

____

____

____

Does your product address any perceived problems—that is, problems that may be associated with image, self-understanding, or some intangible issue? (Again, list as many as you can think of!)

____

____

____

What other *products* are available that address the real and perceived problems your product is designed to address? (List your three most-relevant competitors.)

____

____

____

What are the half-dozen *most common purchase criteria* (in addition to price) that buyers use in deciding which product in your market to buy? List them.

____

____

____

____

____

____

What other *sources* offer products that solve the same customer problems that your product solves? (Question three above deals with *competitive products*; this question talks about *competitors—the outlets that sell the product.*) List three.

____

____

____

Key Reminders

- Consumers *always* buy to solve a problem.
- Some problems are real and some problems are perceived, but most problems are a mixture of real, concrete problems and perceived problems.
- Many problems contain an unarticulated *image* component.
- Customers go through more-or-less predictable steps in identifying their problem, and in seeking a solution to their problem.
- It is possible to map the stages consumers go through as they make a buying decision.
- Customers don't really buy products, programs, or services —they buy solutions.
- The salesperson with the best *solution* to the problem gets to make the sale.
- The customer alone decides what the "best" solution is.

3

How Does a Sale Unfold?

In the previous chapter, we took a hard look at how consumers move through the Consumer Buying Model—from problem recognition and data-gathering to selecting a product, an outlet, and a salesperson that can solve their problem. The entire focus of chapter 2 was the customer—how they gather data, how they behave, what they do and think in the days and weeks up to (and including) the moment when we first encounter them.

In this chapter, we will look at what happens in the sales process itself. That is, once we meet the customer, how does the sale unfold? There have been a lot of words written about selling, and many of them have overcomplicated the sales process—complicating it almost beyond recognition. Some sales models have steps and sub-steps, back steps, quick steps, and even missteps. Salespeople like you and me find our heads swimming as we try to make sense of the whole mess.

Do not be dismayed. There is a simpler way.

Most sales unfold in a reasonable, logical, and more or less predictable fashion. A sale follows a series of discrete steps. These steps generally occur in approximately the same order. And—if you follow the steps professionally and focus on solving the customer's problem—you have an excellent chance of making the sale.

Later on in our work together we'll devote an entire chapter to each of these steps in turn. For now, let's get an overview of the sales process and see what we can learn.

The Sales Process

The process presented in Figure 3-1 maps the stages of the sales process. Where the Path to Purchase focused exclusively on what was going on with the customer, the sales process examines our responsibilities and challenges as salespeople trying to solve a customer's problem.

Interestingly—despite all the variability in sales—there is a predicable way in which people move down the path to a purchase. There may be minor variations in the process based on the type of product, the nature of the buyer, or other factors, but the process remains remarkably constant across product categories, types of sales, and other variables. Let's take a look.

The Sales Process

Step One	**Research Prior to the Sale** *How does my product compare to its competitors?* *How do customers use my product?* *What problem—real or perceived—does my product solve?*
Step Two	**Meet and greet** *How do I greet customers in a way that buyers see me as a credible colleague?* *How do I build rapport?* *How do I get customers to invite me into their problem-solving process?*
Step Three	**Discovery** *How do I discover the problem(s) that drove the customer into the market?* *How do I uncover the key purchase criteria that will drive this sale?* *How do I help the customer clarify his/her problem?* *How do I identify solutions that will best solve the newly clarified problem?* *How do I discover the benefits of my product that are most relevant to this buyer?*
Step Four	**Features and Benefits** *How do I present my product, program, or service in a way that I fully "bridge" from the features I have learned to the <u>benefits that the customer cares about?</u>*
Step Five	**Making the Case/Presenting the Solution** *How do I present the solution to the customer's problem?* *How do I use a "trial close" to flush out objections so I can deal with them?*
Step Six	**The Objective is Objections: Dealing with Resistance** *How do I respond when the customer objects to my presentation?* *How do I remember that "An objection is simply a request for more information"?* *How do I circle back to Discovery to uncover the additional facts I need to solve the customer's problem and make this sale?*
Step Seven	**Closing: It's Okay to Ask for the Order** *How can I ask for the order in way that is congruent with our collegial sales model?* *How do we finalize our commitments to each other in a professional way?*
Step Eight	**Following-Up for Ongoing Profitability** *How do I follow-up for an on-going profitable relationship?* *What other problems can I solve for this customer?* *How do I stay in contact to make this customer a "customer for life"?*

Figure 3.1

Let's look at each of the steps in a little more detail.

Step 1: Research Prior to the Sale

This step is transparent to the buyer—it happens before we ever meet him or her. Thorough research is critical to our credibility—and to our ultimate success as salespeople.

In the *Research Prior to the Sale* step, we focus first on our own product. We learn all the features and benefits of our product. We understand the typical customer problems our product will solve, and learn how to present our product as the solution to those customer problems. It's a tremendous job because it takes a while to fully understand all the ins and outs of the product(s) we represent. But we can do it—in fact, we must do it to be credible. And even when we have fully mastered the product(s) we represent, we have only begun our presale research.

The product we represent does not exist in a vacuum. We are selling in a competitive universe where customers have multiple choices to solve the problem or problems that sent them into the market. To be professional salespeople, we have to know our competitor's products at least as well as we know our own.

Among the questions that drive our study:

- What are the strengths and weaknesses of the competitive product versus the product we represent?
- How do the competitor's salespeople sell—and how can we take advantage of that?

- When people buy from competitors, why (and how often) are they disappointed?
- When we lose sales to the competitors, why and how do we lose them?
- How can we mitigate against those ways in which we lose sales—what will our strategy be?

There's a long list of things we need to know, and going out to meet customers without knowing them is dangerous. You may successfully dance around some questions, but eventually you will look like an unprepared idiot. You lose credibility. You make a bad impression. Eventually you lose this sale, and all subsequent sales to the same customer. Don't do it! Do your research prior to the sale!

Step 2: Meet and Greet

The Meet and Greet step is where the Path to Purchase in chapter 2 and the Sales Process Model we are examining intersect. The consumer has done his or her work and is now out in the market visiting and interviewing potential suppliers. You know your product up one side and down the other, and you know even more about the competitor's product.

And now the two of you meet for the first time—the prospective customer in search of a solution to their problem, and you in search of a sale.

It's a critical meeting—if it goes well, the prospective customer leaves believing that you can help him or her solve the problem. They leave ready to let you earn the business. They leave excited to have met you, with the groundwork laid for a good relationship. If the meet and greet goes poorly, they just leave. Period. And forever—far beyond this single sale.

The meet and greet is where you begin to build rapport and credibility, so that the buyers will invite you into their decision making process. Here's where you sell yourself to the prospective customer—if they don't buy you, they likely won't buy your product. Meet and greet is the beginning of the sale—do it well, and you've got a chance. Do it poorly and the customer might still buy your product, but he or she will buy in spite of—not because of—you.

Step 3: Discovery

In the discovery stage of the sales process, you begin to wrap your mind around the prospective customer's understanding of the problem. Why is this customer in the market—what problem is he or she trying to solve? You discover far more than what the problem is, however. You discover how much urgency the customer has about solving the problem, who else is involved in making the purchase decision, and what budgetary constraints guide the purchase.

If, as we said in chapter 2, "Customers buy to solve a problem," then discovery is where you begin to fully understand the problem and the customer's expectation of what it will take to solve the problem. And—though you do not yet give it voice—you begin to match your product up against the problem, to see how well it matches the prospective customer's purchase criteria.

Discovery is where you *name the problem*. And you can't solve a problem you can't name.

Step 4: Features and Benefits

In Step 4 you begin to talk about your product, program, or service. You detail for the customer the features of your product, and then bridge to the benefits that accrue because of that feature. You also need to get the prospective customer's agreement that the benefits you have detailed actually matter to the buyer.

Step 4 is the one laypeople most often envision when they think about selling. In their language, it might be called, "*Talking about the product.*" And—in many regards—they are close.

Close but no cigar.

If we are to do features and benefits well, we will "Talk about the product in a way that *matters to the prospective customer.*"

Step 4: Making the Case/Presenting the Solution

Step 5 is where we make the case that our product, program, or service can solve the customer's problem better than any other option available. We don't have to solve the problem perfectly—perfect solutions are pretty rare, in fact. But we do have to solve it better than anyone else.

To make the case well, we talk and—most important—we listen. We listen to the prospective customer's concerns and misgivings. We deal with those concerns and misgivings by addressing them, not by explaining them away. And—throughout the interaction—we "check-in" with the buyer to make sure we are speaking to their needs, and not just to our own need to hear ourselves talk.

We don't need to convince ourselves—we work for the company selling the product! The key to a successful sale is to for us to make the case for our product so persuasively that the prospective customer buys as well!

Step 6: The Objective is Objections: Dealing with Resistance

Rarely in your sales life will the customer buy from you immediately after you make the case for your product. There will almost always be some objection—from "Let me think about it" to "Your price is too high" and everything in-between.

Do not panic.

An objection seldom means no. It most often means, "Tell me more." An objection is usually a request for more information, so our job in Step 6 is to circle back to Discovery and determine what additional information the buyer needs. We meet the objection by providing whatever additional information the prospective customer seeks, and checking-in to see if we have addressed his concerns. Then we make the case once again that our product, program, or service provides the customer with the very best solution to the problem that sent them into the market in the first place.

Most people panic at Step 6. Objections are not an occasion for panic—they are an occasion for Discovery through probing and questioning. Once you discover the real barrier to the sale, you can deal with it and move on to Step 7.

Step 7: Closing: It's Okay to Ask for the Order

In Step 7 you get to reap the rewards of all the work you have done in Steps 1 through 6. You've prepared well and met the customer in a way that built rapport and credibility. You've listened carefully and detailed the features and benefits of your product, program, or service. You've made the case that you can solve the problem, and you have overcome objections by circling back to gather more information. Now you get to ask for the order!

This is not some mysterious skill, unavailable to any but the most skilled salespeople. It does not require memorizing "101 All-Purpose Closes." You do not need to be a sales guru to close a sale.

All you need to do to close a sale (and we'll explore this in much greater detail in chapter 10) is to follow Steps 1 through 7 faithfully. Then—once you have flushed out and dealt with each of the objections—look the buyer in the eye and say, "Well, what do you think? Should we do business together?"

If you've done your job well, the answer, more often than not, will be "yes."

And (if you get an objection at this point) you already know what to do. Go back to Step 3 and discover what the issue is.

Step 8: Following-Up for Ongoing Profitability

This is the stage where you begin to really cash-in on all the hard work you did in Steps 1 through 7. Some analysts estimate that it costs nineteen times as much to acquire a new customer as to keep a current customer. And you've already done a lot of work to find this customer, to cultivate him or her, to build rapport, and to make the first sale.

So mine the vein you are already working! Look for follow-up sales to the sale you have just made, and seek referrals to other buyers whom your satisfied customer might know. And remember to service the heck out of this new customer, so that you don't quickly lose the customer you worked so hard to gain.

The Key Lesson: Selling Is a Disciplined, Step-by-Step Process

The key point from Figure 3-1 is just this: selling is a disciplined, step-by-step process. If you learn the steps—and discipline yourself to follow them—you will make your share of sales.

This *does not mean that you can script the sale*, because you can't. You may be able to perfectly predict the first thing out of your mouth, but that's the end of scripting. The prospective customer is apt to say almost anything in response to your first comment, and your second comment has to be tailored to his first comment. So scripting is futile.

Which doesn't mean you cannot—or should not—plan. And to successfully plan for the future, you've got to have some idea of where you are now. You have to know what happened in the past to bring you to the point where you now find yourself.

Where the Heck Am I?—The Alice in Wonderland Question!

In *Alice in Wonderland,* Lewis Carroll offers us a great example of someone who is running as fast as she can, but in no particular direction. In the book, Alice encounters the Mad Hatter and frantically asks, "Quick, quick, which way should I go?" The Mad Hatter responds, "That depends—where are you trying to go?" Alice hurriedly replies, "I don't really know!" To which the Hatter responds archly, "Well then, it doesn't really matter which road you take!"

More than a few salespeople subscribe to Alice's model—they madly rush around, hoping that something they do will generate a sale. But they don't know where they are, they don't know where they want to wind up, and they don't know what to do next. A sorry predicament indeed!

David Campbell—former director of the Center for Creative Leadership in Greensboro, NC—wrote a short book entitled, *If You Don't Know Where You Are Going, You'll*

Probably Wind Up Somewhere Else. Brief as it is, Campbell's book provides a useful and cautionary tale about the role of planning in the work of successful leaders and, by extension, successful salespeople.

His entire point is captured nicely in the title of the book: we have to know where we are trying to go in a sale if we want to successfully arrive there. And that's the beauty of the sales process we are reviewing here—it lets us identify and name where we are in our relationship with the customer.

This sales process gives us a map for moving from our first meeting with a customer all the way through the process—even to the point of follow-up contacts after the initial sale. If we pay close attention to the customer—and carefully monitor our own behavior in the sales interaction—we can almost always tell where we are in the sales process. And where we are usually determines what we ought to do next.

The sales process is *not* a cookbook. You can follow the steps exactly and still sometimes not successfully bake (*or* make) a sale, because you have no control over the customer—a major ingredient in the sales interaction. And—like all maps—this one may sometimes have detours that are not detailed on the map. But it will give you some idea where you have been, and prepare you for the steps you need to take to reach your destination.

And that's important because—to paraphrase Campbell—*if you don't know what you are trying to do, you won't know when you have done it.*

If You Miss a Step, You're Out

In baseball, a runner who forgets to tag a base while running the circuit is called out—the run doesn't count. In selling, the same principle applies—if you skip a step in the sales process, you are going to miss the sale. You are out.

You will get way out in front of the customer—way ahead of him or her in the buying process. The customer will feel rushed and not listened-to. You will miss important information and not fully understand the prospective customer's problem. And the customer will call you "out"—out of the running as a possible supplier, out of the hunt for the sale, out of business, out of a job, out on your butt.

It's called a sales *process* for a reason—you and the customer *proceed* from the meet and greet to discovery and problem identification. In the process of asking questions and listening to the customer's answers, you begin (as we saw in the flow chart) to present yourself as a credible partner in solving the customer's problem. You also build rapport—a rapport that encourages the customer to invite you deeper into his problem-solving process.

Once you fully understand the problem—and not a moment before—you can begin to talk about your product. And as you talk about your product, remember to talk only about the features and benefits that truly matter to this customer. Don't give him or her a laundry list. Review only the attributes that will help this customer solve the problem that brought him into the market in the first place, because that's what builds your credibility as a salesperson focused on service.

Once you have done a good job outlining features and benefits, you are ready to consolidate all your features and benefits and make the case that you—and your program, product, or service—can solve the customer's problem better than anyone else. Building on the credibility you have established by following the process, you present the solution and wait to see what happens.

And sometimes that is all it takes. The customer looks at you in gratitude and says, "Sounds good to me. Let's do it!" In this case, the customer has closed himself or herself. You make the sale and immediately begin the work to ensure that you over-deliver on every promise you made during the sales interaction.

And that's all there is to it.

Sometimes.

More often, though, you carefully make the case for your solution, only to encounter a comment that runs along the lines of, "But what about..." And here's where we reach the heart-stopping objection section of our sales process—the one that strikes fear into the hearts of salespeople everywhere.

All of them except *you*. You're prepared. You've read this book. You know that objections are a normal part of the sales process. You don't panic. You simply circle back to the Discovery portion of the process and ask questions —*discovering* what exactly has raised the customer's concern. And once you have discovered the root cause of the concern, you address it—first with relevant features and benefits, then with the solution you present when making your case.

If—at this point in the sales process—you get more objections, deal with them. If not, this is the point in the process to *ask for the order*! Then follow-up, so that the customer gets exactly what you promised, and becomes a source of repeat business (and steady referrals) for years into the future.

The sale is the pay-off for following the process—for going step-by-step through a disciplined track that takes you from the beginning of the sale to a successful conclusion. The key is to follow the process. If you skip a step in baseball, you lose the run. If you skip a step in selling, you lose the sale. It's as simple as that.

You have to earn the right to move to the next step.

If you skip a step, you lose the sale. Fair enough, you say—that makes sense to me. And it does—most of us can follow steps when we know what the steps are, why the steps matter, and what the consequences are when we skip a step.

But you can also lose a sale by moving too quickly from one step to the next one in the sequence. Perhaps an example will illuminate. I'll exaggerate for emphasis…

Let's say you are getting ready to make a high dollar purchase—one about which you know relatively little. Let's assume you are buying a new HDTV and home-theater system. You have done some prepurchase research by reading a couple of enthusiast magazines. But you are still largely baffled by the whole product category. You are going to have to depend on the salesperson to interpret the products to you, and you are going to have to trust the salesperson to help you make a good decision.

You walk into the store, and are met immediately by a nice young man in khaki slacks and a dark blue knit shirt. If his nametag is to be believed, his name is "Chris." You exchange names, and describe in very limited detail what you are looking for, and the nature and extent of your pre-purchase research. Then Chris begins to ask you questions about your needs—using your name about every third word, and intimating that you and he are best of friends. He is friendly to the point of nauseating—you just met the guy five minutes ago! You begin to feel uncomfortable, and leave the store after about ten minutes, vowing never to go back there again.

What happened?

Chris rushed the process. And it cost him a chance to make the sale.

Look back at our Sales Process Flow Chart (Figure 3-1) from earlier in the chapter. Examine the box labeled "Step 2: Meet and Greet" paying special attention to the three questions detailed in that box. What mistake did Chris make?

Chris *assumed* that he could build rapport and credibility simply by calling you by your first name. He did not devote enough time to building his relationship with you, and it cost him the relationship and the sale. He got too familiar too fast, and you became uncomfortable. Like most customers, you didn't want to make a scene or correct him in person, so you just left. You lost the chance to make a purchase, and he lost the chance to teach you what he knows. All because he tried to rush through Step 2 so he could get on to Step 3.

So what's the point you should take away? Just this—you have to earn the right to move to the next step. And only the customer can decide if you have earned that right. You earn the right to move on to the next step by addressing all the issues that are specific to the step in which you find yourself. And—since you can't read minds—you find out if the customer is ready to move to the next step by asking them.

Now it wouldn't make a lot of sense to say, "Well, it looks like we have finished our meet and greet activities from Step 2 of the sales process. Do you mind if we move on to Step 3?" Your customer doesn't even know there is a process, must less which step you are in. But they do know when they feel uncomfortable. And they do know when they feel rushed. And they do know when they don't feel heard.

So—when you ask them for permission to move on—couch it in language that will feel familiar to them. To move from meet and greet to discovery, it might sound something like this: "Do you have any more questions about my background? If not, let me begin to get an idea of what you are looking for…"

You earn the right to move on to the next step in the process by doing all the work in the step you now occupy. If you're unsure, ask the customer. He or she will know if it is time to move on.

That's All There Is to It!

The sales process has a fair number of steps, but it's not rocket science. If you can cook—or if you can assemble a new purchase using the directions that come in the box—you can follow this process to make a sale. It's not a black box and it's not unlearnable. You want to learn it and I want to teach it. So let's do a quick review of the content, see how it applies to your circumstances, and move forward!

Getting Down to Cases: A Quick Content Review

Alright folks, it's money time. Let's do a quick review to see what you learned. Feel free to flip back through the chapter if necessary, then answer the following questions.

1. In which step do we meet the customer? __________

2. What are the three key things we need to do in this step if we are to build a good foundation for the balance of our interaction? __________________________

3. In which step do we begin to ask questions about the customer's problem? __________________________

4. What happens if we skip a step in the sales process? ________________

5. Is it possible to script out everything we will say in the sales interaction ahead of time? ________________

6. At what step do most people panic? ________________

7. Rather than panic, what should we do when we encounter objections? ________________

8. Some people estimate that it costs ______ times as much to generate a new customer than to hold onto one you already have.

9. There is a step called "Discovery" (Step 3). What do we discover in Discovery? ________________

10. Most products have dozens of features and benefits. Which ones do we stress in Step 4? ________________

11. What step comes after "Making the Case"? ________

12. See Step 8. Why is it so important? ________________

____

____

Key Reminders

- Selling is a disciplined step-by-step process.
- If you follow the steps professionally—and focus on solving the customer's problem—you have an excellent chance of making the sale.
- The fact that most people move down the path to purchase in a predictable way *does not mean you can script the sale,* because you can't.
- To successfully plan for the future, you've got to have some idea of where you are now.
- If you don't know what you are trying to do, you won't know when you have done it.
- Skip a step and miss a sale: Selling is like baseball—if you miss a base in baseball you are out. If you skip a step in selling, you are out!
- You have to earn the right to move to the next step.

4

Identifying Hot Buttons and Flagging Landmines

As we have seen from the Path to Purchase, the sales process begins long before the salesperson and the prospective customer shake hands for the first time. By the time he or she encounters a salesperson, the prospective customer has already:

1. Had an inkling that it may be time to make a purchase,
2. Probably gathered *some* information on the potential product offerings in the marketplace, and
3. Gone to the effort to come to your place of business, or call you and invite you to their home or place of business.

The customer is already at work, doing the legwork necessary to be an informed and intelligent buyer.

As professional salespeople, we owe our potential customers the same amount of preparation that *they* put into their purchases. And we should *never* make them do our homework for us.

Here's a story to illustrate: Many years ago I was the senior sales and marketing executive for a medium-sized automotive products company. One day I got a call from a sales rep—a fellow who wanted to sell me advertising space in the magazines he represented. He *also* wanted me to do his research for him. I was younger and meaner (more handsome, too!) than I am now, and this was not a pretty phone call:

Sales Rep: "Good morning, Mr. McNair, this is Lane Closure with XYZ Automotive Publications. How are you?"

Me: [Exasperated—I've got plenty to do without chatting up sales reps!] "I'm fine. What can I do for you?"

Sales Rep: "I represent XYZ Automotive Publications (he already told me that; how bad does he think my memory is, anyhow?) and I've called to discuss your advertising program. Tell me a little bit about where you are advertising now?"

Me: [Frustrated—this guy wants *me* to do *his* homework for him!] "No thanks. I tell you what: you do your homework and find out where I'm advertising, then call me back with a proposal that will work better than what I am already doing. Thanks and have a nice day. Good-bye."

Sales Rep: [Stunned silence] "Um…good-bye…"

What went wrong here?

Perhaps this rep just called on a bad day. That's always possible—some folks say I can be difficult, and I have no real rebuttal. And no salesperson has any control over whether a given day will be a bad day on the prospective customer's end. But this salesperson also made the fatal mistake of going in unprepared: he had not done his homework. And he expected me to do his work for him.

What should this sales rep have known or have done before picking up the phone and making his telephone call to me? For a start, he should have reviewed the files of his publication (and all relevant competitors) to get a feel for how much and what type advertising my company had done over the past five years. That would give him some idea of our magazine advertising budget, and how it was allocated. Then he could have surveyed all of my company's relevant competitors to see if any one of them was mounting an advertising blitz that my company might need to counter.

The unprepared rep could have polled others in the industry about industry trends, relative strengths or weaknesses for my company, and anything else he could uncover. He could have called someone in our ad agency, asking for an opportunity to meet and discuss his publications. He could have attended an industry trade show and come by our display booth—uncovering additional information about our business and how we went to market.

This seems like casting a wide net, and it is. But when you are doing research prior to a sale, *nothing you learn is wasted*—if it doesn't help you on this sale, it will help you on the next one. If it's not germane to this customer, it will be germane to the next one.

The Implicit Contract between the Buyer and the Salesperson

There is a two-sided, implied contract in the relationship between professional salespeople and their customers. From the customer's perspective, the implied contract goes something like this:

> "If you will help me find the appropriate product and service to meet my needs, I will consider buying it from you. I am willing to answer your questions, but it is not my job to teach you my business, or to educate you on your competitors, their products, or the relative merits of their products versus yours. You get paid for making the sale; *do your own work*."

This contract between the buyer and the seller also has a salesperson's perspective, and it goes something like this:

"I am happy to help you find the product and service that meets your needs and solves your problems. It is my job to sell my product, so you can expect me to include sale of my product in the solutions I propose, but if you out-and-out don't need my product, I will tell you so.

I promise to listen carefully to your problems and your concerns, and to keep confidential all the information you provide to me.

I expect of you the following:

- That you will tell me the truth about your situation and your challenges,
- That you will not waste my time and effort by engaging me just to fill out your need for "three competitive bids" when you have already made up your mind which supplier to use,
- That you will keep my information confidential, and
- That you will pay your bills—in full and on time."

You may have noticed that the salesperson's portion of the contract contains over twice as many words as the buyer's portion of the contract. There are several reasons for this.

First, you are learning how to be a salesperson, and it's your job to learn how to look after yourself. Second, the salesperson usually invests *more in the relationship* than does the buyer—especially up front. The pay-off comes when the sale is made. I am simply trying to clarify the things you have a right to expect, and prevent you from over-investing in prospects who are wasting your time. They *do* exist.

You may be wondering how to use this contract. I'm certainly not asking you to whip it out in the first thirty seconds of a customer interaction. That said, it is important for people to be clear with each other from the beginning of a relationship; clarity can save a lot of wasted time, false starts and—ultimately—frustration. So here's the bottom line: be clear about what you can deliver and ask the buyer to be specific about his or her expectations! Then be clear about your expectations of the customer. You're a professional. You're not chopped liver. You have a right to your expectations every bit as much as the buyer has a right to his or hers.

Identifying Hot Buttons

One of the reasons that presale research is so important is that—as sales people—we want to have some idea of what draws customers to our product or service. We want to know the *hot buttons*.

In the language of selling, "hot buttons" are the product attributes that excite customers and energize them about buying your product, program, or service. These are the *sizzle* that goes with the *steak* of the product you are selling. In some cases the hot buttons are literal attributes of the actual product or service; in other cases they are the less-tangible "coolness factors" associated with the product.

Here are examples of hot buttons for several different products, jobs, or services; take a look and see how they help you identify the hot buttons for the items you take to market.

• Hot Buttons for a house—Houses have an almost limitless number of hot buttons. We will spend an entire chapter (chapter 6—*Discovery: Questioning for Results*) learning how to identify the specific hot buttons that relate to the particular customer you are serving, because hot buttons are never generic. Hot buttons are always unique to the particular customer you are serving.

That said, some relatively common hot buttons relating to home sales include: safety of the neighborhood, layout of the house (as it matches the client's needs), and relative age of the appliances, paint, roof, and heating systems. Other hot buttons include the number of square feet in the house, appearance of the landscaping, proximity to good schools, and so on.

• Hot Buttons for an insurance policy—It's hard to get people excited about insurance—who wants to spend lots of time pondering his or her own death? That's why so many people ignore this portion of their financial planning. Still, there are hot buttons that apply to life insurance. The hot buttons include savings benefits of whole life insurance (this way the buyer may actually enjoy his or her expenditure without having to die), protection for those the purchaser loves, forced investment, comparative internal rate of return versus competitive policies, and so on.

• Hot Buttons for a job teaching school on the island of Saint Thomas in the Caribbean—A friend of mine has a young daughter who is teaching on the Caribbean island of Saint Thomas. The pay's not great, but the weather is wonderful and the view is magnificent. And—as you will see from this quote—the intangible coolness factor is off the chart! Gretchen wrote her parents, "By the way, Mom and Dad, I'm coaching the swim team at Antilles High School. The school doesn't have a swimming pool, so we swim laps in Magen's Bay. *How cool is that?*"

• Hot Buttons for tickets to a concert or sporting event—Tickets to a concert or a sporting event are a good example of something that carries with it significant tangible and intangible hot-buttons. The tangible hot buttons are the opportunity to attend the event—to hear and see the performers, to watch the contest. Another tangible hot button is the chance to network and hobnob with other, like-minded fans of the group or the team in question. The key intangible hot button is the opportunity to bask in the reflected glory of whichever team or group is performing, and the exclusivity of having tickets to an event that ultimately sells out.

As you can doubtless see, *every product has multiple hot buttons*—things that excite the buyer about forking over hard-earned cash for the product, program, or service in question. One of our jobs as professional salespeople is to know the general hot buttons for our product and for all our product's relevant competition.

In the discovery portion of the sales interview our buyer will tell us the specific buttons that matter to him or her. Only when we fully understand our buyer, our product, and the competitive environment in which our product exists can we serve our customers by helping them make an informed choice.

Flagging Landmines

Most of us have seen enough old war movies to understand what a landmine is—it's a hidden explosive that only detonates when you pass over the top of it. Interestingly, sales interactions also contain landmines. A sales landmine is a hidden piece of information that, when you stray across it, carries the danger that it might blow your sales opportunity completely away.

In the example from early in this chapter, the magazine sales rep strayed across a landmine when he uncovered my irritation at his lack of preparation and customer research. Interestingly, that guy never called back. If he had—and if he was prepared—I would have listened to his pitch. I'm a *sales* guy—I like sales people who are prepared, professional, and know what they are doing. I have even bought from sales people just because they were good, even if I didn't really need the product. But you have to be prepared. You have to know what you are doing. And you have to know where the hot buttons and the landmines are.

So what are the generic landmines in a sale? How do we prepare? Interestingly, the landmines in a sale are harder to discern prior to the sale than are the hot buttons. There are generic landmines that might apply in many situations, but the best way to uncover the specific landmines that apply to the sale you are chasing is to question carefully and listen closely to the answers. (You'll learn more about that skill in chapter 6.)

For the meantime, here are ten landmines that you can watch out for as you question carefully and listen closely. Generally applicable landmines include:

1. Previous bad experience with the company you represent.
2. Previous bad experience with the product you represent.
3. Previous bad experience with *you*. You can't remember them at all, but—if their experience was bad—*they remember you.* And it ain't pretty!

4. Unarticulated loyalty to a competitor's product or service.
5. Commitment to buy from someone else (the customer is using you as a second or third bid or estimate just to keep the auditors/boss happy).
6. Embarrassing fact (for example, bad credit) that the customer does not want to reveal.
7. Conflict between two parties on the buying side. (Wife favors you and your product; husband favors a competitor's product and says, "But honey, I know a lot more about this than you do!" A fight is getting ready to break out here. I don't know who is going to win this fight, but it's not going to be you!)
8. Talking to the customer far above—or below—his or her level of understanding. In the first case (speaking above their level of understanding) you lose them. In the second case (speaking below their level of understanding) you irritate them because they think you are being condescending to them.
9. Addressing your comments to the half of a couple that you *assume* will make the decision, and *guessing wrong!* Just because he's a guy, that doesn't mean he is the decision-maker on cars. Just because she is woman, that doesn't mean she will make the decision about the stove without input from him.

It's easy to make the same type of mistake in business-to-business selling—just because one person has the higher organizational title, that doesn't mean he or she will make the decision. You have to do your homework to find out who the true decision maker will be.

10. Assuming that you know (without probing) the issue

that has driven this customer into the market. Don't assume—that's the landmine! *Ask!*

Where Do I Find out All This Stuff?

Hot buttons! Landmines! You are wearing me out, buddy! Where am I gonna learn all this stuff? Plus, I've got a product to sell—I haven't got all day.

Hold on, this stuff is not as hard as it seems.

Let's begin with hot buttons, and let's begin with *you.* You sell the product—what excites you about it? Literally, I mean. Don't regurgitate some crap from the sales brochures. Tell me—in plain English—what excites you about your product. If you can't think of anything, then change product lines. It's impossible to sell something if you can't get excited about it yourself. So make a list of your own hot buttons then ask your colleagues and teammates what excites them about the product, and why it excites them. This is an especially good list, because these are people who live with the product every day. If they don't know why the product is exciting, who would?

All of this preparatory work is, however, just a forerunner to *talking to customers*—the people who really buy and use the product every day. These are people with choices —they don't *have* to buy your product. They could use a competitor's product just as easily as yours, so there must be some reason they have chosen yours. Find out what their reasons are, and log them in your memory so you can refer to them as you sell your product.

The same counsel goes for landmines—what are the places you would be mostly likely to trip up or blow up if you were buying your product? Note 'em, list 'em, and then remember 'em. Then move on to a similar list from your sales colleagues—they likely have some landmine experiences that you have not had yet. Be sure to talk with customers, too. Their experience counts for far more than yours or your fellow salespeople—they actually buy and use the product!

Getting Down to Cases: A Quick Content Review

1. Quick now—what is a hot-button? ______________

   ____

2. Same question, different topic. What's a landmine?

   ____

3. Review the list of ten landmines found in this chapter. Which three do you think are the most relevant for your circumstance? ______________

   ____

4. What are the risks inherent in not doing good presale research? ______________________

   ____

5. Think of the last product you bought that really excited you. Name four hot buttons that moved you to make the purchase you did. ______________

Making It Real: Applying What You've Learned to the Product You Sell

Let's talk about the product you sell—the one that feeds your family and ensures your future. Then answer the questions below about hot buttons and landmines that apply to your product.

Hot Buttons

What three things excite you most about the product you sell? Why are you excited about these three things?

1. ______________________________
2. ______________________________
3. ______________________________

Talk to your colleagues—what things excite them about the product? Pay special attention to the things your colleagues cite that you have overlooked! Why are they excited about these things? How can you plug into this excitement when you talk to prospective customers? Put three of your colleagues' hot buttons below.

1. ______________________________
2. ______________________________
3. ______________________________

Now engage some customers or prospective customers—why do they get excited about your product? These are the people who are willing to give you *their* money to get *your* product—the things they think important are, indeed, *quite* important. Since these hot buttons are at least twice as important as yours or those of your colleagues, list six of them below.

1. ______________	4. ______________
2. ______________	5. ______________
3. ______________	6. ______________

Landmines

Remember that it is harder to recognize landmines than hot buttons—that's why they wind up destroying the sale. With that as backdrop, identify two landmines that you think could cause a sale to jump the track.

1. ______________________________
2. ______________________________

Ask your colleagues about landmines—what has jumped up and bitten them on the butt in the middle of the sale? When have they been taken by surprise and blown completely out of the water? Get two more landmines from them, and list them below:

1. ______________________________
2. ______________________________

Now move on to live customers—a place where you may have to approach this question obliquely to get any useful answers. Asking directly will probably not yield landmines—you may get objections (which we will cover in detail in chapter 9) but you won't get true landmines. Try an indirect approach. Something like, "What about this product or solution doesn't pass the sniff test? What about this raises your skepticism, or makes your bullshit meter go over into the red?" These are critical—if the sale jumps the track here you are out of luck. Enter four customer landmines below.

1. ______________________________
2. ______________________________
3. ______________________________
4. ______________________________

Key Reminders

- The sales process begins long before the salesperson and the prospective customer shake hands for the first time
- When you are doing research prior to a sale, nothing you learn is wasted.
- It ain't the customer's job to do your research for you.
- Be clear about what you can deliver and ask the buyer to be specific about his or her expectations!
- Hot buttons create excitement for the product and move the customer toward the purchase.
- Every product has multiple hot buttons
- A sales landmine is a hidden piece of information that—when you stray across it—carries the danger that it might blow your sales opportunity completely away.
- An objection (chapter 9) is not a landmine. Landmines are more oblique and harder to surface—which is why they are so dangerous.

5

You Never Get a Second Chance to Make a Good First Impression

Like two great streams that flow along in parallel—finally converging to produce one tremendous river—the Path to Purchase and the sales process converge at the meet and greet portion of the sales process. It's in the meet and greet that a salesperson first gets to make contact with a prospective customer. And it is in the meet and greet that potential sales are often cut down before they have even had a chance to quicken and to come to life. These potential sales die because of the way salespeople *meet* their customers —because of appearances and first impressions.

While visiting a client, I once saw a sign posted in the customer service department of the organization. Here's what the sign said:

> *"Using the jawbone of an ass, Samson was able to slay a thousand men. In like manner, we kill a thousand sales every day!"*

Is your jawbone the "jawbone of an ass"? Does the way you meet customers run them off permanently and irretrievably? Or do you meet customers with a *service* orientation, and have them leave that first meeting believing that you have their best interests in mind?

Better yet, how do you know that the answer you have given is right? Do you solicit input from the customers who do not buy? Or is all your feedback from the people who decided to buy? It's a skewed sample isn't it? Perhaps we'd do well to examine—in a little more depth—the fundamentals of meeting and greeting customers.

Barney Fife Was Right!

The Andy Griffith Show has become something of an American cultural icon in the years since it appeared. Andy went on to star in *Matlock*, among other things, and Ron Howard (Opie in the original series) has had a prolific career since his small town beginnings in Mayberry. But of all the people in the large ensemble cast of *The Andy Griffith Show*, Don Knotts—as small town deputy sheriff Barney Fife—seems to have most captured the public's imagination.

Full of bluster and balderdash and blarney, Barney strutted around the sheriff's office like a bantam rooster on steroids and too much coffee. He had an aphorism for every occasion, and never lacked for confidence in his brash and outrageous counsel. He was obnoxious for sure, but it was—if this is even possible—a good obnoxious.

In one particularly memorable episode, Barney is giving counsel to someone who will soon be interviewing for a job. He reminds the job seeker, "Be sure to polish the backs of your shoes—it's the last thing they'll see on your way out the door, and *you never get a second chance to make a good first impression*!"

Barney was often full of blarney, but in this case he was also right. You never do get a second chance to make a good first impression. And—as we saw when looking at the Path to Purchase in chapter 2—the meet and greet is the only opportunity you have to make that good first impression. You'll have, if things go well, many more occasions to spend time with this customer—many more opportunities to confirm their good judgment in choosing to work with you. But there will never be another chance to meet the customer again for the first time.

You've Got to Care about Your Customers

Think about your own experiences when you are buying something—especially a high-dollar item that you know relatively little about (a new computer, a surgeon for a major medical procedure, a new heating/air-conditioning system for your home, etc.). You and I personally—and customers in general—have widely divergent emotional responses to this situation.

Responses can range far and wide, including:

- **Sometimes we are excited:** the new item will save us money, or make our lives easier, and we can't wait to make the purchase.
- **Sometimes we are anxious:** we don't know much about this purchase (selecting the surgeon, for instance) because we face this choice infrequently, and anxiety is consequently our dominant feeling when we move out to make our choice.
- **Sometimes we are baffled:** there is just too much to know, and we can't even decide where to start.
- **Sometimes we are even irritated:** we made a poor choice when buying last time (or we were treated badly in the purchase) and we are irritated that we have to go through the whole process all over again.

In every case, the first thing we are looking for is a salesperson who authentically *cares* about us and about our circumstances. We seek someone who will take the time to understand the situation surrounding the purchase, and then walk with us through the situation to our ultimate decision. We seek someone we can trust, someone with credibility, someone who can partner with us in making the best possible decision.

Trust is the fundamental factor in the equation, and trust is built on a salesperson listening to—and connecting with—the customer. Credibility follows trust (no trust = no credibility), and credibility is built on a salesperson's breadth of market knowledge. Neither trust nor credibility alone is sufficient—the two must exist simultaneously if a salesperson is to make the case that she or he is the best possible partner in making a decision.

To put it simply, *Customers don't care how much you know until they know how much you care.*

Where Are We in the "Path to Purchase"?

As a salesperson, it is critical that we *always* know where we are in the Path to Purchase, because where we are drives what we do next. By the time we meet and greet a customer, he or she is already well on the way to making a purchase decision. As you can see from Figure 5-1, the consumer could be as far along as Step 7 in the buying process.

The prospective customer may well have identified their need (Step 1), gathered some preliminary data (Step 2), and clarified their need (Step 3). They may even have identified possible options to meet the need (Step 4), developed their purchase criteria (Step 5), thought about potential sources (Step 6), and perhaps even contacted multiple possible sources for their potential purchase (Step 7). You may not be the first salesperson to whom they have spoken—they may already have visited with several other salespeople before they shake your hand.

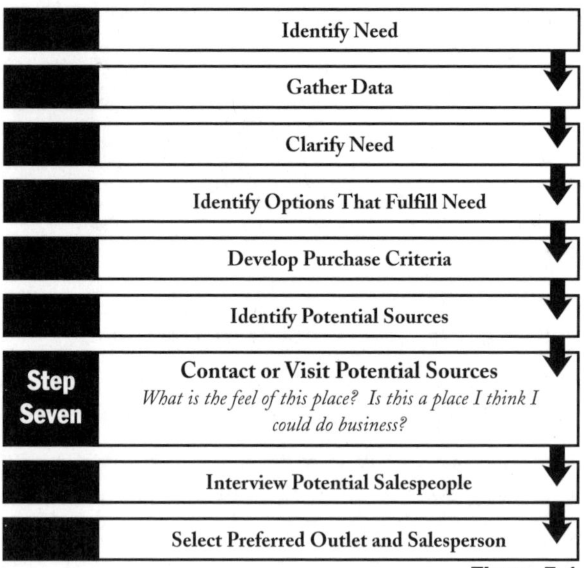

Figure 5-1

In fact, it is in soliciting possible sources for purchase (Step 7) that we most often meet prospective customers for the first time—whether in a query phone call, or in an in-person meeting. The customer is very often way ahead of us—he or she has already been thinking about his or her problem and the best possible solution for that problem. Our challenge is: 1) to get her or him to envision us as the best possible source/supplier for solving the problem, and 2) for the two of us to begin to move together down the path to the final purchase.

So we pick up the customer after he or she has done lots of internal work reflecting on the sale. They are near the end of the Path to Purchase—one of the two streams that converge to create our sale. The other stream is the sales process, and we'll likely find ourselves much closer to the beginning of that process. Let's take a look...

Where Are We in the Sales Process?

When we make our initial contact the customer is well along in the Path to Purchase—they may be as far along as Step 7. However, they are only at Step 2 in the Sales Process, as shown in Figure 5-2 below.

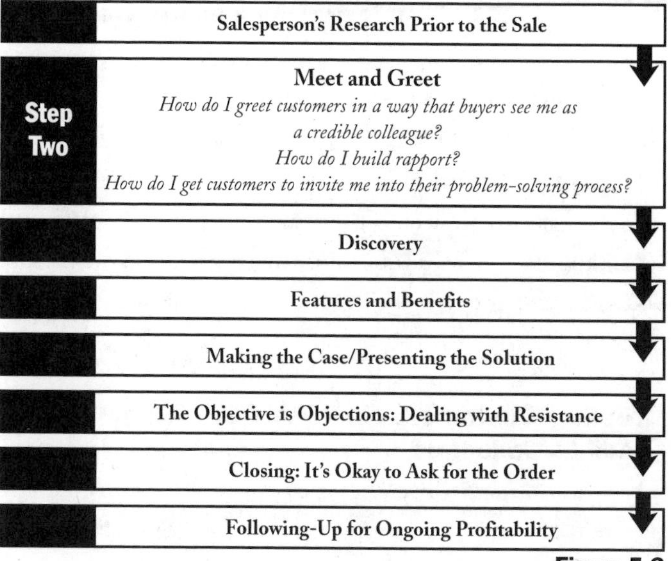

Salesperson's Research Prior to the Sale
Step Two
Meet and Greet
How do I greet customers in a way that buyers see me as a credible colleague?
How do I build rapport?
How do I get customers to invite me into their problem-solving process?
Discovery
Features and Benefits
Making the Case/Presenting the Solution
The Objective is Objections: Dealing with Resistance
Closing: It's Okay to Ask for the Order
Following-Up for Ongoing Profitability

Figure 5-2

Our Challenge in the Meet and Greet

Our challenge in the Meet and Greet is to—at the very least—address the three questions posed in Figure 5-2 as Step 2:

1. How do I greet customers in a way that they *see me as a credible colleague*?
2. How do I *build rapport*?
3. How do I get customers to *invite me into their problem-solving process*?

These three questions are additive, meaning that question two builds upon question one, and questions one and two support question three. Put differently, customers have to see you as a credible colleague (question one) before they are willing to develop rapport with you (question two). They must experience you as credible (question one) and have rapport with you (question two) before they will invite you into the process that solves their problem (question three).

Greeting Customers So They See You as a Credible Colleague

There are so many different types of people—with so many different styles of communicating and ways of relating—that it may seem impossible to speak in general terms about how to present one's self as a credible colleague. It's not.

Think about the questions you carried into your last interaction with a salesperson—questions you have when *you are the buyer*. I don't know all of the questions you had, but I'd bet these were among them.

- Does this salesperson listen to me when I talk?
- Is this salesperson willing to get to know me before trying to sell me? Am I a human being, or just another "turn at bat"?
- Does this salesperson know what he or she is talking about?
  Their own products and applications?
  Competitor's products and applications?
  The differences between—and similarities of—the two?
  The advantages and disadvantages of each?
- Does this person move the process along at a pace that feels comfortable to me?

Most customers go into *most* buying situations with many of the same questions you take into your own purchases—including some or all of the questions above. To establish ourselves as credible, we have to generate favorable answers to these questions. That is, we must value the customer as a human being—as someone beyond just our next opportunity to make a sale. We must, for sure, know our stuff. And we must let the customer set the pace of the buying experience. And—especially—we must *listen*! Let's look at these one by one.

Building Trust through Listening

Trust is one of the key dimensions of the sales process. Buyers rarely buy from sellers they do not trust. Trust that allows the prospective customer to tell you the truth about the problem that brought them into the market, and trust helps them buy the solution that you offer in response to their problem.

So what is it exactly that builds trust?

Sadly, there are many schools of selling that focus on ingratiating oneself to the customer—sucking up to them in a way that makes them your "new best friend" or bosom buddy. Except for the most naïve of customers, this stratagem is not usually successful.

Trust in relationships takes times to build, and usually accrues when the salesperson demonstrates to the buyer that he or she can be counted on—that she or he can be relied upon to do some or all of the following:

1. Tell the truth—the whole truth—without shading it to advantage,
2. Listen carefully to the customer's problem(s),
3. Question closely to ensure he or she fully understands the customer's circumstances and buying constraints,
4. Respect the customer—the customer's desires and needs and constraints,
5. Educate the customer—if the seller knows things that will help the buyer make an informed decision,

6. Partner with the customer—so that both the buyer and the seller get a solution that works for each of them, and
7. Shape a solution that solves the customer's problem within the constraints laid out by the customer.

Clearly, all of these steps won't transpire in the first two minutes of the meet and greet. But the groundwork for all these steps can then be laid. It all begins with customer-focus and a willingness to listen to the problem or problems that brought the customer into the market in the first place. There are no techniques or tricks to facilitate the building of trust—rather, trust develops when we encounter our prospective customers with a focus on them, not us—an authentic desire to help them meet their needs and achieve the goals that brought them into the market. Let's take a look.

It's Not about You!

Too many salespeople think that the Meet and Greet is all about them.

You may know some of these salespeople—they fall into the trap of seeing the meeting with the customer as a stage and their interaction with the customer as a performance. So what the customer gets is an act—the salesperson *acts* interested, *acts* friendly, *acts* truthful—all in pursuit of ingratiating him or herself to the buyer. This acting would be bad enough even if it was effective. But it isn't.

Ernest Hemingway once said that the fundamental requisite to write good fiction was a "built-in, shock-proof bullshit detector." (That is, people have to know it when they write, or read, or hear a true sentence.) Most people have a bullshit detector—buyers included. And they can smell a phony—a salesperson focused on him or herself, rather than the customer—from a mile away.

Play-acting with customers is not only bad drama—it's bad selling!

The key to a successful meet and greet is not ingratiating yourself to the buyer, it's listening to—and caring for—the buyer. That is, don't act interested—*be* interested. Don't act honest—*be* honest. Don't act respectful—*be* respectful. Amazingly, if you move into the sales interaction with a focus on serving—not selling—the customer, these outcomes will occur effortlessly and as a by-product—you won't have to create them at all.

Selling is not about you—how bright you are, how cute you are, how manipulative you can be. Selling is about the customer—how carefully you can hear her, how well you can serve him, how faithful you can be in solving the problem that brought the customer into the market in the first place.

Building Rapport

Where trust is a foundational thing—a bedrock on which to build a relationship—rapport is less substantial and more fleeting. Surely in your life you have known or worked alongside people with whom you had some rapport (they were fun to chat with; you found them engaging) in spite of the fact that you did not have enough information to know whether or not to trust them a great deal. You probably have many relationships like this even now—casual workplace friends, wait staff at your favorite restaurant, the letter carrier on your route, etc. You like them, you have rapport with them, but you don't know them well enough to have an opinion about trusting them with something important.

That is why we began our meet and greet discussion with trust—in an ideal sale, it should always precede rapport. Still—rapport matters. So how do we build rapport?

Generally rapport grows from *shared experiences, values, backgrounds,* or *interests.* Which is why you often find salespeople trying to chat you up—they are looking for points of connectedness that will allow them to claim some sort of rapport with you.

Sadly, much of this chatting builds what I call *faux* rapport. That is, the salesperson is so desperate for a connection that he or she will say anything to claim a connection—one that may not really exist. The salesperson is a Packer Backer today and a fan of the Cowboys tomorrow. A Democrat when selling to Democrats and a Republican when selling to Republicans. And this is where the customer's bullshit detector begins to go off.

Fortunately, there is a solution. And it's easier than you think…

Rapport is built—at least in part—on overlapping interests. Think of the folks with whom you most enjoy spending time—the ones with whom you have *rapport*. What central interests do you have in common? I'll bet there are several—or at least one fundamental one. Maybe you share a hobby, an interest in a particular athletic team, or the same religious tradition. Whatever it is, this commonality of interests is a major contributor to the ease you feel with each other—the *rapport* that sustains your relationship.

And it's the same way in sales. You don't have to lie to build rapport—you and the customer already have the most important commonality you could possibly claim. The customer has a problem that your product, program, or service might be able to solve. You are both interested in this deal, because—if she or he buys your product—you have both reached an important goal. You've made a sale, and they've solved their problem. This is enough commonality on which to start a relationship. And this is true commonality—not some trumped-up commonality based on allegiance to athletic teams you may or may not support in real life.

Get Invited to the Problem-Solving Party!

Let's recap—we're thinking about what happens when we meet and greet a customer near the beginning of the sales process. We've set ourselves three objectives for this stage: 1) establish credibility, 2) build rapport, and 3) get invited into the problem-solving process. And we've examined in some depth how to establish our credibility and how to build rapport. How in the world do we now get invited into the customer's problem-solving process?

I've got some good news. If you do the things we have just identified, you've already done what it takes to get invited into the prospective customer's decision-making process!

If you establish yourself as credible by what you know and how you listen, *if* you develop a bond of trust between yourself and the client, and *if* you build authentic rapport based on your shared desire to solve the customer's problem—if you do these faithfully and thoroughly—you'll get invited to help solve the problem. You've got to sell yourself before you sell your product. And—if you do—you'll get an opportunity to make the sale! In fact—if you do all these things well and authentically—you are guaranteed an invitation to the Problem-Solving Party. Because these are the things that build rapport and trust—and who wants people you can't trust at a party of any sort?

It's as simple—and as challenging—as that. You don't have to do a song-and-dance, you don't have to schmooze, and you don't have to ingratiate. But you do have to listen, you do have to know what you are talking about, and you do have to build trust and develop rapport. Do all these things, and you are on the short list of salespeople invited to help solve the customer's problem.

Cold Calling—A Special Type of Meet and Greet

Much of what we have talked about so far has been pointed primarily towards sales situations where the customer seeks out the salesperson to make a purchase (automotive sales, real estate sales, a host of others). Many, many purchases fit into this category: the buyer moves through the steps of the Path to Purchase, and then eventually steps out to begin an encounter with a salesperson.

But there is a whole other world of selling—the world of cold calls, of dialing and smiling, the world of picking up the phone (or going door-to-door) to generate prospective customers for a product, program, or service. And it makes sense to deal with cold-call selling here and now.

Before we go further, let's establish one irrefutable fact about selling as it regards cold calls. There are only two kinds of people in the world: salespeople who say they hate cold calls, and salespeople who lie!

Cold calling is hard, hard work—it has a high rejection rate and requires someone with thick skin and a well-developed sense of self-confidence. Prospects are much more likely to act like jerks and treat the salesperson badly, and they feel justified in acting this way because they have been interrupted in whatever they were doing to respond to the salesperson's call.

Prospects are also very impatient in a cold call—the salesperson has to "hook" the prospect's interest in the first thirty seconds (on the phone) or the first couple of minutes (in person), or the conversation will go no further. In some ways, the first few sentences of a cold call become like the headline of an advertisement—if the headline doesn't grab the reader, the game is over. If the first couple of sentences don't grab the prospect, the cold call is over. This is why you find cold call securities salespeople asking you, "Would you like to double your return on your investments?" It's also why cold call sales spiels often lead with an amazing claim, a gripping story, or an astounding fact—anything to hook the prospect and keep him or her in the conversation long enough to begin the steps we have talked about here.

There are no tricks to minimize the prospect's initial irritation—it's a simple fact of life. No one likes to be interrupted. The key to overcoming this irritation is to give the prospect a reason for the interruption—a benefit so important ("doubling your investments returns") that the irritation is suspended or dissipates. And that's why cold calling salespeople almost always lead with the most astounding benefits of their product—to grab the prospect's attention.

Here's the little-known fact about cold calling—once you have the prospect's attention, the sales process is exactly the same as the one we have been describing. You meet the prospect at Step 2 (see Figure 5-2), and move through the process in the very same way you would have moved through the process if the prospect had sought you out in your place of business. It's the same process, with the only difference being that you start in a one-down position because you have interrupted (and likely irritated) the prospect in the way you first met each other.

But once you have met and "hooked" the prospect by piquing their interest and attention, you are back in the flow of our normal structured sales process. You move through the tasks of the meet and greet by establishing credibility, creating trust, and building rapport. And once you have done all three of these things, the customer will invite you into his or her decision making process, and you can begin the discovery phase of the sale—a phase that we will discuss in detail in out next chapter.

Cold calling appears more to be more different from other selling than it actually is—after the initial hurdle of a different way of meeting the customer, the steps are the same. Occasionally—as we noted—prospects will be irritated by the interruption of a cold call. You either "hook 'em" and overcome their irritation, or they remain irritated and you move on to the next prospect. Either way you are not burdened for long with their irritation.

Schmucks

Sadly, there is another type of difficulty you may encounter as you meet and greet potential customers. It's time to talk about schmucks. I have saved this section for last because it's not good news. But it is true—and it's my job to tell you the whole truth about selling, so you'll be prepared when you hit the street. So listen up.

Some people are jerks. Get used to it. Don't let it affect your interaction with the next customer.

Ever park your car in a lot and have someone run a key down the side and scratch it from hood to trunk? That was a schmuck. Ever see some obviously healthy person park in a handicapped parking place, then leap out of the car and race into the mall? Another schmuck. Ever see a customer publicly berate wait staff at a restaurant—for the quality of the food, not the service? Yet another schmuck.

Unfortunately, folks like this also buy the products you sell, and occasionally you'll meet one of them. They will do all the things I have counseled you not to do: they will lie to you about prices from other suppliers, they will hammer you in conversations with your management, they will misrepresent things you have said in your conversations with them.

It is difficult to deal with people like this—they can ruin your faith in all of humankind. And a major caution is in order: *Carbondum non illegitimiti!* (Don't let the bastards get you down!)

It is difficult to deal with folks like this—I know because I've met them. But you can also learn some key lessons in dealing with them. Here are several lessons I've taken away; perhaps they will be helpful to you:

1. *Never say something* to a customer that *you wouldn't want repeated on the local television newscast.*

2. *Put it in writing*—whatever "it" is. Your commitments, their commitments, your agreements, their agreements—write them down!
3. *Keep management in the loop*—as soon as you realize that you might be dealing with a schmuck, let your manager know. The best defense is a good offense.
4. *Refuse to sell them.* I saw this work very well when I worked at a major consumer products company. We had a few customers who were clearly committing fraud in returning our products for credit. We kept records, and eventually wrote them a "do not buy from us because we clearly cannot meet your needs" letter. It's a last resort, but it is one trick in your bag. Don't forget it. It can save your sanity.
5. *Don't let it get you down.* The same world that produced the jerk you are dealing with produced Mother Teresa and a host of saints and heroes too long to list. Move on. Don't get stuck in the negative.

So there it is—Meet and Greet—the first face-to-face encounter in the sales process. This encounter is the foundation of all that follows. If it goes well and you build authentic rapport, you'll get invited to the problem-solving party. If it goes poorly and the prospective customer does not trust you or find you to be credible, you'll be drinking alone. It's important to master this step if you want to play the game at all, so let's review key reminders and see how they apply to the selling you do.

Getting Down to Cases: A Quick Content Review

Let's take a moment and check in. What have you learned? Where are we? How can you apply the material you have just reviewed? Answer the questions below, then we'll review some key reminders from this chapter.

I have never believed that life was a closed book exam—I'm more interested in what you can learn and apply than in what you can memorize. For each question, you'll find one or more page references that can help you answer it correctly.

1. In the meet and greet portion of the sales process, two things converge. What are those two things? (See page 75) ______________________________

2. When customers arrive at the meet and greet, what stage of the Consumer Purchase Cycle are they most likely to be in? (See pages 79–81) ______________

   ____

3. When consumers arrive at the meet and greet, what stage of the sales process are they in? (See page 81)

   ____

4. What are the key challenges of the meet and greet stage of the sales process? Name all three. (See page 82) ______________________________________

5. The chapter names seven things that help build trust between a salesperson and a prospective customer. List your four favorites below. (See pages 84–85)

____

6. What has to happen for the salesperson to get invited into the prospective customer's decision-making process? (See pages 88–89) _______________

____

7. How is the meet and greet in a cold call different from the meet and greet in other sales situations? (See pages 90–92) _______________________

____

8. How are cold call sales similar to other sales? (See pages 90–92) _______________________

____

9. What is it about cold calls that irritates the prospective customer? (See pages 90–92) _______________

10. What is a schmuck? What is the most important thing to remember in dealing with a schmuck? (See pages 92–94) _______________________

Making It Real: Applying What You've Learned to the Product You Sell

The questions above were all about the chapter—and that's all well and good. You bought the book to learn how to sell, and you can't learn if you don't read and master the chapter. That said, it's not what you *read* that makes the sale. It's what you *do*. So let's explore some questions about what you do when you meet and greet your customers.

1. When you meet and greet a customer, what is your number one objective?

2. What do you do to help yourself accomplish this key objective?

3. After reading this chapter, how will you handle the meet and greet differently?

4. What mistakes do you see others make when they meet and greet their customers?

5. What is the worst thing that a salesperson has ever done when meeting and greeting you in a sales interaction?

6. What is the single most important thing you learned in this chapter?

7. How are you going to use what you have learned?

Key Reminders

- As a salesperson, it is critical to know where we are in the Path to Purchase, because where we are drives what we do next.

- The Path to Purchase and the sales process converge in the meet and greet.

- Our challenge in the meet and greet is to address these three questions:
    1. How do I greet customers in a way that they see me as a *credible* colleague?
    2. How do I build *rapport*?
    3. How do I get customers to *invite me into their problem-solving process?*

- You and the customer *already have the most important commonality* you could ever claim—the customer has a problem that your product might be able to solve.

- *Sell yourself* before *you sell your product.*

- You never get a second chance to make a good first impression.

- To be a successful at cold calling, you have to have a "hook."

- Some people are jerks. Get used to it. Don't let it affect your interaction with the next customer.

6
Questioning for Results

Take a moment and remember a time when you were miserably sick. Not a life threatening illness—just the wretched routine of a horrific cold or an exhausting bout with the flu. You have tried for a couple of days to tough it out and get well on your own, but to no avail. You can't breathe, you have fever and chills, and your hair hurts. You surrender and decide to see what the doctor has to say.

The front desk staffer greets you, gets a quick review of your symptoms, and ushers you to the waiting room. In a surprisingly brief period, you are called to an examination room where you flip idly through old magazines and play with a reflex hammer lying on the countertop. The wait seems interminable.

Finally you hear a rustle in the hall, and the doctor bursts into the room, stethoscope draped around her neck. "So, I hear you've been a little under the weather," she says. You take a breath to respond, and are interrupted before you can frame your first sentence.

"You look terrible, but then there's a lot of this going around. I bet I've already seen a half dozen cases this morning," she continues. "You'll just have to ride it out for a couple of weeks." She whips out a prescription pad and her pen scratches across the paper. "Here are a couple of prescriptions that ought to tide you over. That ought to do you. Hope you feel better soon." And she is out the door before you have a chance to speak—let alone to protest.

You put your head in your hands and ask yourself: *Did this actually happen?* She did not ask you a single diagnostic question. In fact, you didn't even have to be there for this "interaction" with the doctor—there was no interaction. "That ought to do you," indeed! You certainly feel done, that's for sure!

So what is wrong with this picture? There are many things wrong, but first among them is this: our physician has violated a key tenet of good patient care—always diagnose before you prescribe. She assumed she knew what was wrong with the patient—and that is a critical mistake in medicine and in selling.

Further, our attending physician did not gather any information from the patient. This is a mistake on two levels: input raises buy-in, so a patient is most likely to follow a treatment plan that she or he helped design. Further, the patient is closest to the illness and people never argue with their own facts—it makes sense to get those facts early in the case.

Differential Diagnosis

A key skill taught in any medical school curriculum is the ability to do what physicians term *differential diagnosis.* That is, the ability to differentiate one disease from another, even if the diseases have the same set of presenting symptoms. And—to do differential diagnosis precisely—the critical skills are the ability to *question precisely* and to *listen carefully*.

An example: a patient appears at a hospital emergency room with a terrible stomachache. The patient is doubled over in pain—curled into a fetal position, lifting his head only to give brief one-word answers to questions posed by the attending physician. What could possibly cause this acute abdominal pain?

A good first guess would be appendicitis. But guessing is not the best tactic in medical diagnosis (or in sales, for that matter!) Another possible option would be an ectopic pregnancy, but observation seems to indicate that our patient is male, so that option appears out.

And so the physician begins a series of questions designed to pinpoint a specific diagnosis by eliminating some possibilities and focusing more clearly on others. Among the questions the patient is likely to hear:

1. Have you ever had this pain before? If you have had it, what caused it then?
2. When did the pain first begin?

3. Have you had any other symptoms, such as nausea, diarrhea, or bloating?
4. When was your last bowel movement? Was it normal —whatever that is for you?
5. Have you ever had appendicitis? Have you had your appendix removed?
6. Do you have any food allergies?
7. What have you eaten in the last twenty-four hours? Anything unusual or new to you?
8. Have you had a blow to your stomach? If so, when was it? How hard was it?
9. Do you have any diseases of the digestive system?
10. Have you had a recent physical examination? Did any concerns come up in that exam?
11. Has anyone ever told you that you have a hernia?
12. Has a physician ever mentioned to you that you might have an abdominal aneurysm?
13. Are you taking any medication? Any medication for diseases of the digestive system?
14. Have you begun any new medication of any type in the last three days?
15. Is there anything else I should know that would help me treat you?

In the first couple of minutes of the interaction, the medical professionals have asked over twenty questions in fifteen distinct question blocks. All of this in pursuit of more fully understanding this overarching, implied question of the patient: What brings you here today, and how might I be helpful to you?

Clearly, this is a book for salespeople, not medical students—else I would be woefully unqualified to write it. Even so, the question above is the fundamental question underlying the initial interaction between any salesperson and a prospective customer. We absolutely need to know the answer to the question *"What brings you here today and how might I be helpful to you?"* before we have a prayer of helping customers find the product or service that meets their needs and solves the problem that sent them into the market in the first place.

Where Is Discovery in the sales process?

Discovery happens very early in the interaction between the salesperson and the prospective customer. Technically, discovery is Step 3 in the sales process, as shown in Figure 6-1. In actual practice however, Discovery often begins in the early moments of the Meet and Greet (Step 2, see below).

Let's take a look now at the Sales Process Model and see where the formal Discovery step falls in our process.

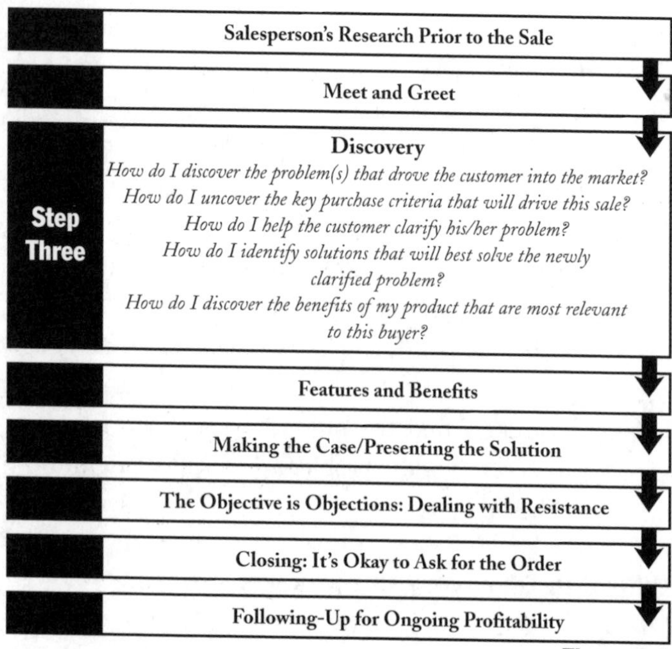

Salesperson's Research Prior to the Sale
Meet and Greet
Step Three
Discovery
How do I discover the problem(s) that drove the customer into the market?
How do I uncover the key purchase criteria that will drive this sale?
How do I help the customer clarify his/her problem?
How do I identify solutions that will best solve the newly clarified problem?
How do I discover the benefits of my product that are most relevant to this buyer?
Features and Benefits
Making the Case/Presenting the Solution
The Objective is Objections: Dealing with Resistance
Closing: It's Okay to Ask for the Order
Following-Up for Ongoing Profitability

Figure 6-1

As the salesperson and the prospect chat and build rapport, the prospect often volunteers key information about where he or she is in the sales process. You may hear things like: "You're the third salesperson I've met with today," or "Gosh, I hope your prices aren't as high as the last guy's prices were!" Even as you are meeting and greeting the prospective customer, you are discovering information that will help you when you begin to define the problem that brought this customer into the market.

As an example, let's look at the two snippets of information we just uncovered. What do we know if we know that we are the third person he or she has met with today? Well, we know a lot. Among other things, we know:

1. This customer is being purposeful about this purchase. They have contacted multiple vendors, and are interviewing prospective suppliers.
2. We are not the first salesperson they have talked to—they already have a frame of reference from the two earlier salespeople.
3. The previous conversations have probably helped them clarify their purchase requirements—they likely have a better understanding of the specs for this purchase than they did when they began their interviews of with prospective salespeople.
4. They probably already have prices from at least one of the earlier salespeople. You need to find out what prices they already have so you can gauge where you need to be so you are in the range on price.

There are many other things we could conclude from a comment like, "You're the third salesperson I've met with today" but I don't want to belabor the issue. What I *do* want to point out is that—as a salesperson—it is never too early to start gathering data (to *discover* something) about the sale you are trying to make. The meet and greet is a fine place to begin!

Remember our credo from chapter 2: people buy to solve a problem. A problem (or a perceived problem) sends every prospective buyer into the market, every time. No exceptions. And the salesperson who presents the "best" (remember: *the prospect defines best!*) solution to the problem gets the sale. Every time. No exceptions. Ever.

Our job in the Discovery portion of the sales process is to use targeted questions to identify the problem that sent our customer into the market, and to determine what the prospective customer sees as the "best" solution for the problem. We then present a solution—one that uses our product or service—that fits the prospect's "best" template. Voilà! Happy customer, problem solved, sale made, money in your pocket. Questioning is where it all begins.

How Questioning Works

So how does questioning work in actual practice? Let's take a look.

Buying a car is an almost universal experience in our culture. Most of us have done it at least once; many of us have done it half a dozen times. So let's assume for a moment that you sell cars. How does the Discovery portion of the automotive sales experience usually unfold?

Before you put on the mind of an automotive salesperson, I want you to reflect on your experience as a customer. You (as the customer) begin with the notion that you need to do something about the car you now have. (Or about the fact that you do not now have a car.) You find yourself reading the car ads in your local newspaper, and you begin to actually watch—and listen to—the commercials you see on television. Perhaps you buy a *Consumer Reports* so you can get unbiased reporting on the types (economy car versus mid-sized, for instance), brands (Honda, Chevrolet, et al.), and models (Accord, Malibu, so forth) of vehicles available in the market.

As a buyer, you have entered the problem-recognition and data-gathering stages of the Consumer Buying Model found in chapter 2. Most customers—for most products—do at least some of this work before they ever go out into the market and meet a salesperson. Generally, the more expensive the product (cars, homes, computers) or the more important it is to the customer (athletic equipment, high-end audio goods, expensive appliances, etc.) the more research the customer will do before he or she ever hits the market.

Even in this day of online purchasing and 1-800 phone lines, most customers eventually have to go to a retail distribution point to kick tires, twist knobs, or click a computer's mouse. And that's where the salesperson's professional questioning skill—the ability to do *differential diagnosis*—comes to the forefront. Let's chase our car-buying example a little further, and see how on-target questioning can help both the salesperson and the customer understand exactly what the customer needs and wants.

For the next few moments, you are a professional automotive salesperson—let's give you a job at the local dealership.

You have worked at this dealership for a number of years, and you are a professional. That is, you know both your own and the competitors' product lines, you work continually to hone your skills as a salesperson, and you believe that the best sale is the one where the customer and the salesperson both leave happy.

You are hard at work making follow-up calls to last week's contacts when you notice a couple has just walked into the dealership. You leave your desk to meet and greet them, and as you walk towards them you notice that they are wearing wedding rings, and that they seem to be in their early thirties. You kept in mind an old admonition from one of your mentors—*assume nothing!*—and begin to frame some questions that might apply to these prospective customers.

You also remember the overarching question that informs Discovery (*What brings you here today, and how might I be helpful to you?*) as you frame your questions. You don't have long—the couple is only thirty feet across the dealership floor from where you sit—but half a dozen questions pop quickly into your mind. The questions (and the background behind them) include:

1. Good morning, how can I help you? *(This question lets you know why they are here. They may be here to visit another salesperson or to pick up a car they have already purchased. Or they just may be your next satisfied customers!)*

2. Have you visited our dealership before? Have you ever bought a car from us before? *(Gives you insight into how much they know about how your dealership does business. Do you need to sell the place, or just the vehicle?)*
3. What type of vehicle were you thinking about? *(Helps you determine which—of the 500+ cars on the lot—to begin with as you present products to them. Also gives you an idea of the price range in which they are shopping.)*
4. Who will be driving this vehicle most often? *(Can help you decide to whom you should address the majority of your conversation. Can also get you in trouble if you confuse the user with the buyer—since they are not always the same person!)*
5. Did you have in mind a new vehicle or a used vehicle? *(Again—helps you decide where to start. Gives you some idea about their budget.)*
6. How many people will normally be in the vehicle at one time? *(Gives you insight into the size of vehicle they seek, and whether children are part of the mix. If children are involved—and these two people are the parents—safety will be an important feature of any vehicle you present.)*

As the young couple answers your questions, you *discover* a number of things about them—all useful as you begin to determine how you might be helpful to them. For this example, you discover the following things:

- They are not here to meet someone else, and they have never visited this dealership before—you have to sell the dealership as well as the vehicle.
- They are married, but not to each other—they are actually brother and sister.
- The car is for the woman; her brother is accompanying her because she wanted some help in the purchase and—as she said—her husband "doesn't know jack about buying a car!"
- The woman is the mother of three children under the age of eight. She is a stay-at-home mom who is home-schooling her kids—she is looking for a minivan that will also serve as a homeschool bus.
- She wants to buy a new vehicle for the dependability and warranty, but money is an issue because hers is a one-income household.
- She has a six-year-old sedan that she wants to use as a trade-in, and she is very interested in some of the rebate programs she has seen advertised—including the owner loyalty cash incentives.
- She intends to keep the car a long time, so it does not matter to her if she buys a current-year model or a close-out model from the previous year at significant savings off the sticker price.

As you can see, every question helped flesh out the profile of the prospective customer and helped the salesperson (that's you!) understand "what brought them here and how you might be helpful." We'll explore this specific story again later; for now let's take a few minutes to reflect on the types of questions we can ask when we are doing Discovery, and the mechanics of framing and sequencing questions in the Discovery process.

Question Types: The Difference—and Why It Makes a Difference

There are two fundamental types of questions we use in sales: open questions and closed questions. You are already familiar (even if you don't know it) with each of these types of questions from years of using language in everyday conversation, but let's define them just for the sake of clarity.

Open questions are the "essay" questions of life—they require a paragraph answer. They often begin with words or phrases like:

- "Tell me about"
- "Explain"
- "What happened when"
- "Why"
- "How"
- "How do you feel about"

Open questions are useful because they "open up" a topic—giving the salesperson a range of useful information that can be used to help craft a sale. Open questions can also be used to "open up" a particular kind of buyer—getting the non-talkative person to share information, ideas, and issues that will affect the eventual sale.

Let's take a look here at a sample open question about a customer's trade-in vehicle. We'll contrast the information discovered through an open question with the information garnered from a closed question on the same issue.

Open and Closed Questions

The conversation has moved to discussions about the prospective customer's trade-in vehicle, and the salesperson asks a simple open question: "Tell me a little about the vehicle you will be trading in?"

The customer replies: "We'll be trading in a 1999 mini-van. It has about 110,000 miles on it, has never been wrecked, and has been dealer-maintained since the day that we bought it new. It has full power and we recently had it professionally detailed to get it in tip-top shape for trade."

See how much information the salesperson got with one simple, open question? We now know how often the customer trades cars, how many miles he or she drives in an average year, how he or she cares for their vehicle, and what type vehicle will be involved in the trade. Open questions are famous for "opening up" a topic—they give you lots of information and have the added advantage of encouraging the customer to talk.

Let's now see how the salesperson did with a closed question about the same trade-in...

The conversation has once again moved to discussions about the prospective customer's trade-in vehicle, and the salesperson asks a simple closed question: "Do you anticipate trading-in a vehicle when you buy this new car?"

Customer's reply, "Yes."

The salesperson does know more than before this question, but not much more. This was a situation where a closed question did not do much to advance the sale—the salesperson did not learn much, the prospective customer did not talk much, and the relationship between the two did not grow much. An open question would have been a better choice for this situation.

Of course—and this is the great thing about selling—*you have more than one chance to get it right*. The salesperson could follow his less-than-useful closed question above with an open follow-up question and still wind up with the information needed to advance the sale. Perhaps our sales friend could chase the customer's simple "yes" with an open query like this: "Well then, tell me a little bit about the vehicle you'll be trading-in."

Open questions have several pluses: they get lots of information (some of it unforeseen), they get the customer to talk, and they provide a more conversational interaction than a series of closed questions. So, why don't we confine ourselves to open questions only? Because open questions are not perfect.

Open questions can take a lot of time, and they can be inefficient if you are dealing with someone who talks a lot. Furthermore some people can manage to answer even the best open question with a grunt—leaving you no better off than if you had asked a closed question in the first place.

The best use of closed questions is often after you have gotten to know the customer—having already built trust and rapport. You can then use closed questions to quickly review options on the vehicle, like paint colors, radio/stereo options, etc.

The takeaway is: either type of question can be effective in helping you understand the answer to the key sales question: *"What brings you here today, and how might I be helpful to you?"* The fundamental issue is not what questions you ask, or how you frame them. The fundamental issue is this: do the questions you ask help you identify the problem the customer has come here to solve?

If your questions do this, you're in business. And if they don't do this, then work on them. It is nobody's fault but yours if you aren't ready with good questions in your first meeting with your customer. It's not like you're surprised that someone has come in to buy from you—you sell for a living! And you know that you have got to do Discovery to get to the close.

The Probing Question—So Easy It Ought to Be Illegal!

In addition to open and closed questions, there is also a powerful questioning type called a probing question.

Although most probing questions could also be categorized as open or closed, they are a separate category because of their unique uses in gathering information.

Probing questions are used to gather additional information about a topic that is already on the table. The purpose of the probe is to encourage the speaker to keep talking, or say more about the issue at hand. We (salespeople, doctors, therapists—anyone who listens for a living) often use probing questions to extend our understanding of the topic, or to cast a wider net and keep reeling in information from the talker.

You may be wondering why this section has the subtitle "so easy it ought to be illegal." The answer is quite simple: probing is very easy. By far the biggest challenge for the listener is to keep his or her mouth shut while encouraging the speaker to keep going. Here are some sample probing questions; you may have others that you especially like:

- Are there other concerns you have about this?
- Is there anything else you'd like to add?
- What else comes to mind?
- Is that all?
- Go on…
- Tell me more…

Remember: the focus of probing is to keep the other person talking, so you can gather more information and they can heighten their buy-in. Probing is also a useful way to clear up issues when you are unclear what the prospective customer meant by a comment—keep them talking and you will usually understand in time.

Probing is a powerful tool: *When in doubt, probe!*

Questioning Patterns: Funnels, Tepees, and Hourglasses

The types of questions you ask are critical, but so is the order in which you ask them. There are several questioning patterns that occur as we gather information from our prospects. We'll review three common questioning patterns, and reflect on an example of each. You'll find that each of the patterns has a name that suggests very much how the pattern looks and works. The important thing to remember is to vary the way you ask questions—*choose* your questioning pattern intentionally, rather than falling into a comfortable questioning pattern by default. Each questioning pattern is appropriate in some situations—none of them is appropriate in all situations.

The Funnel Questioning Pattern

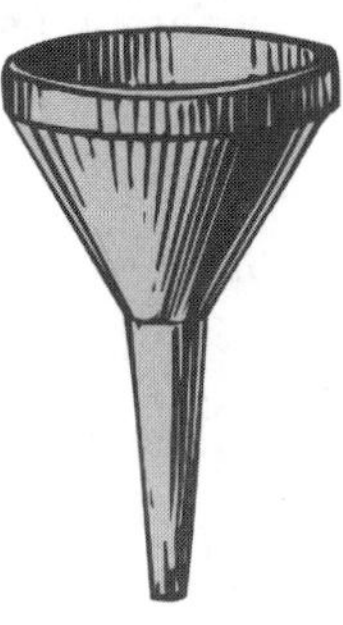

The Funnel Questioning Pattern begins with one or more open questions, and then narrows the focus as the salesperson and the prospect begin to zoom in on the issue as hand. As an example, consider the scenario that began this chapter—the encounter at the doctor's office. Let's assume that our sample physician takes a much-needed course in effective questioning and listening.

In that case, she might use a questioning pattern that went something like this:

Question 1: How are you feeling today? (A very open question.)

Question 2: Tell me about your symptoms? (An open question but focused solely on symptoms.)

Question 3: Have you been nauseated? (A closed question.)

Question 4: Have you had a fever or chills? (A closed question.)

Question 5: Have you experienced any muscle weakness or aches? (A closed question.)

The funnel pattern moves from the general to the specific—casting a wide net at the beginning of the conversation, and then narrowing focus as the interaction continues, and as the questioner learns more about the circumstances of the person answering the questions.

The Tepee Questioning Pattern

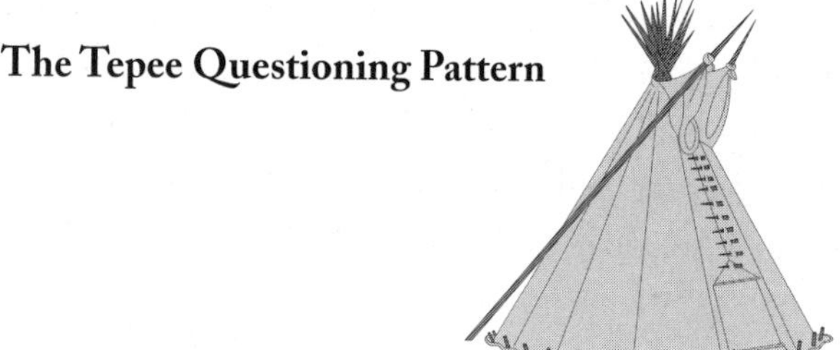

The Tepee Questioning Pattern is the exact reverse of the funnel pattern: it begins with one or more closed questions and then opens up as the key topic comes into focus. As an example of the Tepee Pattern, consider the following questions a highway patrol trooper might ask a motorist pulled over for a traffic violation.

Question 1: Do you know what the posted speed limit is? (A closed question.)

Question 2: Do you know how fast you were going? (A closed question.)

Question 3: Do you have your license? Can I see it, please? (Two closed questions.)

Question 4: Do you have your vehicle registration and insurance card? Can I see them, please? (Two closed questions.)

Question 5: Have you been drinking? (A closed question.)

Question 6: Please tell me about your consumption of intoxicants in the last twenty-four hours? (An open question with a specific focus.)

As with the funnel pattern, the focus here is not on how you ask the questions—the focus is on getting the information you need to help the prospective customer define and solve the problems that brought them to you in the first place.

The Hourglass Questioning Pattern

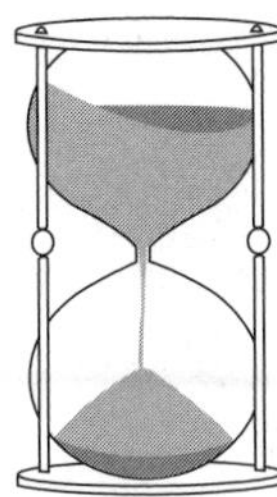

The Hourglass Questioning Pattern is a marriage of the Funnel Pattern and the Tepee Pattern. It most nearly represents how a real conversation between buyers and sellers would progress. The conversation begins with an open question or two, then moves to closed questions as the focus narrows. The closed questions identify another issue of concern, and the pattern swings back again to one or more open questions. Consider the following example from our automobile scenario earlier in the chapter.

Question 1: Good morning, how can I help you? (An open question)

Question 2: Tell me a little about what you are looking for in a new car. (An open question)

Question 3: Tell me some of the things that you like best in your current car. (A closed question—really just seeks a list of attributes)

Question 4: Do you want air conditioning in your new car? (A closed question)

Question 5: Do you want a sunroof? (A closed question)

Question 6: Do you want or need four wheel drive? (A closed question)

Question 7: You mentioned that you occasionally use your current car as a towing vehicle. Will you want to use your new vehicle to tow as well? (A closed question)

Question 8: Tell me about the towing you do with your current vehicle. (An open question—focused on towing.)

Question 9: What kind of towing will you do with this vehicle? (An open question—focused on towing.)

The hourglass pattern captures the natural ebb and flow of sales conversation—from open questions to closed ones and back again to open. Remember that the primary objective is to get the information you need to solve the customer's problem and make the sale. Questions and questioning patterns are important—you have to know how things work to use them appropriately. But the fundamental objective is to understand the problem that brought the customer to you, and to determine how you can solve that problem so that the customer can get what he or she wants and you can make a sale.

Question Families

In addition to the types of questions (open, closed), questions also come in "families"—that is, questions can be grouped into clusters, with each cluster addressing the same basic subject. Although the subjects vary widely from industry to industry, there is a broad range of question-topics that can apply to almost any purchase. All of the following are question families (there are doubtless many in addition to these) and each family can contain multiple questions.

- Reputation/Perception (of manufacturer, product, salesperson, etc.)
- Price (gross and net)
- Cost (not the same as price—includes price of maintenance, hassle, etc.)
- Financing (often part of the sale in consumer durables; critical in real estate)
- Productivity/Efficiency (more applicable in business-to-business selling, but applies to many consumer products as well: air conditioners, microwaves, lawnmowers)
- Quality (includes many measures: dependability, durability, etc.)
- Image (not the same as reputation—more intangible and status-focused)
- Service (availability, quality, and training of service people, etc.)
- Warranty (length, inclusiveness)

- Technology (new or old? innovative or old and proven?)
- Complexity (how hard is it to operate the product?)
- Product Options (how many, what type)
- Purchase Options (what could the customer buy instead of your product?)
- Delivery (how quickly, what cost)
- Uses and applications (single-purpose product or multiple uses)
- Problems (with current product/application; fears of problems with new product)

Some Sample Questions

Sample questions always give me a headache. Not because I can't write them (I can) but because I don't want to hamstring you, or to limit your creativity in framing your own questions. Still, you bought the book. You want to learn how to sell. I promised to teach you. And a list of sample questions can be *very* helpful. So I have some sample questions below—sorted into five sample categories.

Clearly, I could create a hundred pages of sample questions and still not exhaust all the options. But I already know how to create questions. I just want to give you enough examples so that you can create the perfect questions to make the sales you have to make.

Category: Core Problem

- What problem are you trying to solve with this purchase?
- Why did you decide to make this purchase now?
- If this purchase solves your problem, how will things be different?
- How is the current situation affecting your ability to get your work done?
- How do you hope that making this purchase will make things better?

Category: Product Specs

These questions are often very industry- or product-specific. Nevertheless, I wanted you to have a feel for possible questions in this category.

- What is the single most important way you want this purchase to improve on or be different from the product/service you now have?
- What is the single most frustrating thing about the product or service you will be replacing?
- How much output are you looking for from the new equipment?
- How much output are you getting from the old equipment?
- How is downtime with the old equipment?
- How much are you now spending on maintenance?
- What efficiency level do you now have? What do you want?

Category: Competition

- Who else are you talking to about this purchase?
- Have you had any previous experience with this seller?
- What other products are you considering?
- Have you had any previous experience with this brand/product line?
- Do you have references from or for any of the suppliers you are considering?
- Can I give you some references to compare with the others you have?

Category: Price

- How much is your budget for this purchase?
- Have you already committed the money, or are you just testing the market?
- How much did you pay for the item you will be replacing?
- How much is the current item costing you in downtime and maintenance?
- Where does price fit in the list of attributes that will help you make this decision?
- Have you considered total cost (downtime, maintenance, product life, hassle)—rather than front-end cost—as a possible way to make the decision?

Category: Buying Process

- Who else will be involved in making this purchase decision?
- Will any end users of the new product be involved in the buying decision for the new product?
- Could I talk to some end users of the current product?
- When do you anticipate making the buying decision?
- What criteria will drive your purchase decision?
- If a committee is involved in the buying decision, would it be possible for me to meet with all of them?

Back to Selling the Car

Remember our car-sales scenario from several pages ago? Let's return to that situation for a moment and examine how questioning can help you fully understand the customer's problem so that you can develop a solution that works for everyone.

To recap: you are meeting with a thirtyish woman who is a prospective customer. She has brought her brother along to help her make this purchase. The woman has three children under the age of eight, and she homeschools them. Her home is a one-income household, so money is an issue. She will be trading in a six-year-old sedan. She keeps her vehicles for a long time, so she does not care whether the vehicle she buys is a current year model or a closeout from the previous year—the depreciation hit over the life of the purchase will be inconsequential. Your prospective buyer mentioned that she is very interested in some of the rebate programs she has seen advertised on television, as well as low-rate financing offers.

You know what it's like to *buy* a car. Now you get to move to the other side of the desk. Reflect for a moment on the situation above—what do you need to know to solve this customer's problem? What do you need to know to make this sale? Enter your answers below, and do not turn to the next page until you have fully answered each question below.

Information Needed to Solve the Problem *(list at least five things you need to know):*

1. ____________________
2. ____________________
3. ____________________
4. ____________________
5. ____________________

Information Needed to Make the Sale *(list at least five things you need to know):*

1. ____________________
2. ____________________
3. ____________________
4. ____________________
5. ____________________

How'd You Do?

Let's see how you did! I have listed below some things you would need to know so that you could solve this customer's problem and make the sale. My list is not exhaustive—see how many you have that match mine. What did you miss? What did *I* miss?

Information Needed to Solve the Customer's Problem—Partial List

- Length of average trip (regular or extended chassis)
- Normal number of people carried (seating options)
- Average amount of time she spends in this vehicle in a day (seating/entertainment options)
- Amount of "stuff"—groceries, suitcases, athletic equipment—she normally carries (regular or extended length chassis? one or two sliding doors?)
- Importance of access to rear of van (two sliding doors or one)
- Importance to prospect of acceleration and gas mileage (six or eight cylinders)
- Appeal of upscale accessories (DVD player to entertain children, two-zone AC)
- Receptivity to a used vehicle (more options for you as you make sale; lower price)
- Importance of "new" from a warranty standpoint (also gauges receptivity to used)

- Importance of third party reference data (*Consumer Reports*, *Motor Trend*, etc.)
- Type of upholstery wanted
- Importance of good service from selling dealer (warranty work)
- Other vehicle brands (make, model) being considered
- Other vehicle types (SUV, extended cab truck) begin considered
- Special option packages/bundles that might save customer money on target vehicle

Information Needed to Make the Sale—partial list

- Whether this is a cash deal or will be financed
- Trade-in value of six-year-old sedan (down payment amount)
- Whether trade-in is owned outright or still under lien (down payment amount)
- Buyer's credit rating (interest rate, qualification special incentives)
- Amount of financing buyer can qualify for
- Number of miles driven in a year (lease or purchase)
- Price of all cars in the buyer's universe of acceptable alternatives (yours and competitor's)
- All relevant manufacturer's incentives that apply to vehicles this customer might buy (rebates, low-rate financing, buyer loyalty programs)

- All manufacturer's incentives for competitive vehicles customer is considering

It is critical to *know what you need to know* before you begin asking questions. Otherwise, you will miss a key piece of data and the sale will jump the track later on in the process. Don't just "wing it" when you prepare to question—make sure you are purposeful and intentional in determining what you need to know *before* you begin the process of framing your questions. Remember: good physicians always diagnose before they prescribe. And you can't do a diagnosis unless you know what you need to know!

Framing Questions

Okay—you're making progress. Maybe you'll make it in the exciting world of sales after all! You have all the background information from the meet and greet, plus a long "shopping list" of information from the exercise we just completed. Of course, just because you know what you need to know, that doesn't mean the customer will spit it out in a form that is useful to you. You have to frame questions that get at what you need to know, and you have to ask the questions in a sequence that makes sense.

Take a look at the information we examined on open and closed questions earlier in this chapter, and also look at the questioning patterns we reviewed. Then frame half a dozen questions that will take you where you need to go—

six pointed to solving the customer's problem, and six pointed to making the sale itself.

Remember: it is easier to get some information obliquely rather than head-on. You'll probably have better luck with "What other vehicles have you considered?" (an open question about competition) than with "Have you talked to any of my competitors?" (a closed question that sounds mildly accusatory).

Caution: Never ask people direct questions about their credit rating early in a sales interaction—they don't know their rating anyhow, and most people find this question off-putting. You can introduce the question later—perhaps by offering to "check with the credit people and see how low a rate you will qualify for." Then get them to sign the credit authorization and move forward. (The same caution applies in business-to-business selling; the purchaser is not usually the CFO or the accounts payable department. Discuss credit with the people who have control over credit, and that is not usually the buyer!)

Framing Questions to Solve the Customer's Problem

1. ______________________________
2. ______________________________
3. ______________________________
4. ______________________________
5. ______________________________
6. ______________________________

Framing Questions to Make the Sale

1. ______________________________
2. ______________________________
3. ______________________________
4. ______________________________
5. ______________________________
6. ______________________________

Getting Down to Cases: A Quick Content Review

Discovery is a fundamental step in the sales process, and the foundation for all subsequent steps. Take a moment to reflect on all we have talked about—you might even want to flip through the whole chapter again. Then answer each of the questions below as completely as possible.

What are the three most important things you learned in this chapter?

1. ______________________________
2. ______________________________
3. ______________________________

Based on this chapter, what two things—that you have not been doing—will you begin doing when you are in the Discovery portion of the sales process?

1. ______________________________
2. ______________________________

What one thing have you been doing in your selling that you realize—based on what we've learned about Discovery—probably is not helpful? List that thing below, and commit to change it.

1. ______________________________

What are the two most common types of questions?

1. ______________________________
2. ______________________________

What are the best uses for closed questions? __________

____

____

What are the best uses for open questions? __________

____

____

Making It Real: Applying What You've Learned to the Product You Sell

"Discovery" is one of the longest chapters in this book. That is no accident. Discovery is the very foundation of the sale itself. If we don't *discover* the problem that brought our prospective customer into the marketplace, how can we ever hope to solve it? Plus—as you'll see—key things you miss in Discovery don't simply vanish—they just pop up as objections later in the sales process. So Discovery is a fundamental step in the whole sales process.

Let's now move to the program, product, or service that feeds your family. What things do you need to know to solve your customer's problems? There must be dozens—list eight key items below.

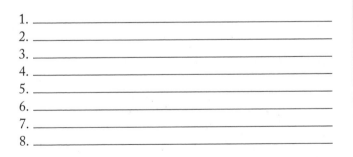

Information I Need to Know to Solve My Customer's Problems

1. ____
2. ____
3. ____
4. ____
5. ____
6. ____
7. ____
8. ____

As we saw in our automotive-sales example, we often need different information to make the sale than we need to solve the problem. In the markets you serve, what information must you have to make the sale?

Information I Need to Make the Sale

1. ______________________________
2. ______________________________
3. ______________________________
4. ______________________________
5. ______________________________
6. ______________________________
7. ______________________________
8. ______________________________

Sadly, most customers don't just walk into our lives and blurt out all the information we need to solve their problems and make the sale. We must carefully craft questions that help us discover the information. Using the space provided below, craft five questions that will help you uncover the information you'll need to solve the customer's problem, and an additional five questions that will help you make the sale.

Five Questions to Solve the Customer's Problem

1. ________________________________
2. ________________________________
3. ________________________________
4. ________________________________
5. ________________________________

Five Questions to Help Make the Sale

1. ________________________________
2. ________________________________
3. ________________________________
4. ________________________________
5. ________________________________

Key Reminders

- People buy to solve one or more problems.
- Solve the problem and get the sale.
- It's easier to *listen* someone into buying than to *talk* someone into buying.
- Always diagnose before you prescribe.
- The key question is this: *What brings you here today, and how can I be helpful to you?*
- Open questions are the essay questions of life—they get your paragraph answers.
- Closed questions can get you lots of information in a hurry.
- When in doubt, probe.

Sales Step Four

7

Features and Benefits: The Difference and Why It Matters

I have been teaching selling for twenty years, and I have been selling for more than forty. Every time I teach selling, the hardest concept for new sales people to grasp is the difference between features and benefits. I don't know why this is, but it's a fact. So here's a heads-up for you; I am going to do my part and work hard to differentiate between features and benefits. You are going to have to do your part, too. Focus, dude, and let's roll...

Here's the simple answer to the difference between features and benefits:

- A feature is an attribute of a product, program, or service.
- A benefit is a reason for the customer to care (and to buy!).

Let's begin our thinking about this topic using some exaggerated examples, then we'll work backwards to the selling you do to feed your family and build your career. In almost every case—for almost every product—there are more features than benefits. And in every case without exception, salespeople are tempted to talk about features, while customers focus on—and buy—benefits.

How Do Features and Benefits Fit into Our Disciplined Sales Process?

Salesperson's Research Prior to the Sale
Meet and Greet
Discovery
Step Four
Features and Benefits
How do I present my product, program, or service in a way that I fully "bridge" from the features I have learned to the benefits that the customer cares about?
Making the Case/Presenting the Solution
The Objective is Objections: Dealing with Resistance
Closing: It's Okay to Ask for the Order
Following-Up for Ongoing Profitability

Figure 7.1

Features and Benefits: The Fire Extinguisher

Consider the ubiquitous and humble fire extinguisher. They are so prevalent that they are almost invisible—like part of the wallpaper. We don't even see them anymore. And unless you have ever used a fire extinguisher to put out a fire, you probably don't think about them much. But fire extinguishers have loads of features and benefits. Let's take a look…

Clearly, there are different sizes of fire extinguishers, with the larger extinguishers better able to deal with larger fires. So size is one feature (remember, a *feature* is an *attribute* of a product, program, or service) of fire extinguishers. There are also different manufacturers, so that manufacturer becomes another feature. And—as with most product lines—some manufacturers are better known and more highly regarded than others.

Fire extinguishers—as you may recall from school fire drills—are rated for various types/classes of fires. Fires are classified as "A" (fires involving paper, wood, cloth, and so forth), "B" (combustible liquids like gasoline and cooking oil), and "C" (electrical) fires. Consequently, another feature of a fire extinguisher is the class(es) of fires against which the extinguisher can be used. Fire extinguishers also differ in their ability to be recharged so they can be used again. So the presence (or lack thereof) of recharge capacity is a fourth feature relevant to fire extinguisher purchase. And then there is price—a feature of every product (including fire extinguishers) that you will ever sell. Clearly—as with all products—some fire extinguishers cost more, some cost less.

There are doubtless other features of fire extinguishers, but let's quit here. This is a treatise on selling, not fire prevention.

Remember: features are characteristics or attributes of a product, a program, or a service. We've identified five features in this example on fire extinguishers. The features are:

1. Size
2. Manufacturer (and reputation of that manufacturer)

3. Suitability for a given class of fire
4. Capacity for recharge
5. Price

Now let's reflect on the benefits that apply to a fire extinguisher: *what does a fire extinguisher do?* Fire extinguishers:

1. Put out fires
2. Save lives
3. Protect our investment in property
4. Keep us out of trouble with regulatory authorities (in many commercial applications like hotels, office buildings, hospitals, manufacturing plants)

It is the last list—not the first list—that represents the key benefits of buying a fire extinguisher. In fact, benefits often relate to the *saving* of one or more of the things enumerated here: lives, money, property, or hassle.

I remember the first time that I discovered the power of benefits in my own selling life. It was a major "ah-ha" for me to realize that—when I spoke of features—I was talking about my product and what mattered to me. When I began to talk about benefits, I was putting myself into the position of the buyer—talking about what mattered to him or to her and speaking to the problem he or she sought to solve. The shift in perspective may seem subtle, but the effect on the sales process (and my sales success!) was profound.

Now let's look at a very different product.

Features and Benefits: The Parachute Example

Have you ever jumped from a plane—skydiving through the clear blue yonder? I haven't yet, but I've always wanted to.

Parachutes can have a raft of features; we'll list just a few. A parachute can feature a quick-deploy canopy—permitting the diver to jump from relatively low altitudes. The canopy can also be steerable, giving the user a fighting chance of landing somewhere close to the intended target (or avoiding the trees and power lines that threaten to make this jump the last jump!)

Further, canopies can be colored—either bright orange for visibility, or camouflage for hiding once the user is on the ground.

Moving beyond the canopy, the harness can be a quick-release harness, useful if you are blown off-course and land in the water with the soggy canopy dragging you quickly underwater. And the shrouds (the lines that connect the canopy to the harness) can have high tensile strength, making them useful for other purposes if you land in the boondocks and have to cut up your parachute to survive.

Again, we have five features out of a possible universe of dozens. They are:

1. Quick-deploy canopy
2. Steerability
3. Canopy color
4. Quick-release canopy
5. Shrouds with high tensile strength

So what are the benefits of a parachute? There are really only two benefits, and both of them have the same core:

1. Parachutes save your life while you are in the air (features one, two, and perhaps three), and
2. Parachutes save your life once you have landed (features three, four, and five).

As in our fire extinguisher example, parachutes have many more features than benefits. But the benefits, not the features, are what the customer buys. Let's look at another product—this time an intangible—to see how features and benefits work in a different context. This time let's take a look at some of the possible features and benefits of a life-insurance policy.

Features and Benefits: Life Insurance (Intangible Products)

Researchers and survey statisticians say that life insurance is one of the most difficult products in the world to sell. To begin with, there is no immediate thrill from spending the money, as there is when you buy a new automobile, home, article of clothing, or even a CD. And the sale of life insurance forces customers to open up and talk and think about two of the major taboo topics left in our culture: death and money.

So what are some of the features of life insurance? As with our other products there are hundreds of features, but let's quickly identify five. First there's the company offering the insurance—some are household names, others new and relatively unknown. There's also the price of the product—often measured in dollars spent per thousand dollars of coverage. Third is the company's rating—several rating firms assess the financial stability of the various insurers, and these ratings can play an important role in driving customer purchase choices.

Next are the terms and conditions of the policy itself—how many weeks or months must you wait before the policy is "in force"? What activities (war, extreme sporting competitions, acts of God) would limit payment under the terms of the policy? What is the savings component of the policy—and what are the interest rates on money that goes into the savings portion of the policy?

And a final feature of an insurance policy is the payment periods—must you pay annually in one lump sum? Can you pay quarterly, monthly, or even weekly? Will the insurer debit your checking account, or must you undergo the hassle of writing and posting a check every time a payment is due?

There are hundreds of ways to slice and dice these features—as you likely know if you have ever had to sit through a sales presentation by an agent seeking your business. In fact, there are so many options that buying insurance is an often-baffling process. Life insurance is truly a product where the competent salesperson *serves* (as we discussed in chapter 1) by offering expertise, guidance, interpretation, and a way through the maze of product offerings and obscure terms.

With hundreds of features as backdrop, what are the possible benefits of life insurance—what is the customer buying when he or she signs an insurance contract and begins writing premium checks? The most obvious benefit is the pay out—what many policies actually refer to as the *death benefit*. The death benefit is the amount of money your heirs or designees get on the occasion of your death.

Cash is a *tangible* benefit, and it's generally the biggest tangible benefit in the life insurance business. The biggest selling point in the life insurance business is rarely the death benefit, however. And this observation moves us to the arena of intangible benefits and their impact on the selling process.

The largest single factor in the sale of life insurance is not the concrete amount of the death benefit. And it's certainly not the payment terms, or even the savings features of the policy. The engine that drives life insurance sales is an intangible: *the desire to care for those people one loves most.* The desire to be a good provider, to secure someone's future.

In these terms, the cash payout/death benefit is just another *feature* of the policy. The benefit is the care one demonstrates for loved ones, plus the ability to meet their financial needs—even from beyond the grave. That's what makes most sales of life insurance. Surely there are other benefits: the ability to shelter money from taxes is a primary one, and there are others. But the Big Kahuna is the intangible benefit of feeling good by securing the future of those we love most.

Intangible benefits often figure mightily in the sale of products that appear to be strictly rational sales. We'll explore this in more detail later, especially as we examine the universal benefits involved in selling, and as we explore (in chapter 9) some of the objections that can arise when we begin to close a sale.

Why do salespeople talk about features when buyers only care about benefits?

Why *do* folks talk about features when customers are only interested in benefits? I have several thoughts about this; here are my most compelling theories.

It's All We Know

Sales training is difficult and exhausting work and most managers—sales or otherwise—aren't very good at it. So they send their neophyte salespeople off with reams of technical data and encourage them to memorize everything they can about the product. The result of this so-called "training" is that salespeople know hundreds of details about their products, but can't articulate a single reason that the details would, should, or could matter to any specific buyer.

We Think We Are *Supposed* to Talk

"Boy, he's a talker!" we say about a child. And the next thing out of our mouth is, "He'd make a great salesperson." Ain't necessarily so! Selling is not so much about talking as it is about listening, clarifying, understanding, and solving problems. (Remember our chapters on research, meet and greet, and discovery?) Excess talking is not an asset in any of these pursuits.

We Are Afraid to Be Quiet

Selling is a scary business. The customer can reject us, reject our product, or both. And rejection is no fun for anyone. Sometimes we talk—about features or anything else we can think of—just to drown out the sound of our pounding hearts.

We Wouldn't Recognize a Benefit If It Jumped Up and Bit Us on the Butt

The biggest reason we talk about features instead of benefits is that we do not know how to bridge from all the features we have learned to the benefits our customers care about. We have memorized all the features and it's all we know. So it's what we talk about. We never give the customer a reason to care. We never solve his or her problem. We just babble away about our product. But the customer doesn't give a rip about our product. The customer cares only about the problem he or she has, and how we might help solve it.

If It Doesn't Matter to the Customer, It Doesn't Matter, Period

Interestingly, there is an easy way to discipline yourself to talk about what matters to the customer. Here's what to do: every time you get ready to make a statement, imagine the customer sitting in front of you, eyes narrowed, arms folded across his or her chest. And imagine that—in response to your remark—the customer replies with a quick and pointed query:

> *WSIGAF?*
> *("Why should I give a flip?")*

We have to give our customers—for every feature we name—a reason to "give a flip." And the only reasons they are obligated to acknowledge are reasons that relate to the problem—real or perceived—that they brought into the sales interaction in the first place.

Don't talk about a feature if you can't make it matter to the customer. Remember: if it doesn't matter to the customer, it doesn't matter, period.

The Universal Benefits: Key Things That Matter to Your Customer

As we saw with our earlier examples of fire extinguishers, parachutes, and life insurance, all products have multiple features. And most products have far more features than benefits. But it's the benefits that make the sale. Fortunately, there are fewer than fifty benefits in the world. These benefits (I call them the universal benefits) drive every sale ever made—now or in the future.

The universal benefits relate to money, power, prestige, self-understanding, fear, and the other core motivators that drive all human behavior. Here's the list as I have been able to identify it:

The Universal Benefits

Make more money	Make a contribution
Spend less money	Make a difference
Save more money	Be heard or valued
Have more money	Avoid pain
Work less/fewer hours	Be vindicated
Save time	Be autonomous
Have more time off	Feel heard
Look good to others	Do competent/quality work
Be attractive	Get recognition/be a hero
Be part of a winning team	Play more
Work with folks I like	Have fun!
Learn something new	Serve God
Use new technology	Serve a higher-order goal
Be more productive	Look good to myself
Have fewer hassles	Be all I can be
Be safe	Reduce risk
Be secure	Be left alone
Save time	Minimize fear

Figure 7-2

Let's take a look at these universal benefits from a practical perspective. How do they work in the real world?

Pick an example. Since I love sports cars, I'll start there. Suppose someone dropped a couple of cool million on me and I could buy any car I wanted. What would I buy and why?

As this is written, I'd likely buy a Honda S2000 coupe, and I can cite at least half a dozen of the benefits above as reasons for buying this car. Take a quick look:

- Fewer hassles—it's a *Honda*, for heaven's sake! Maintenance should be a breeze.
- Have fun!—speaking of breeze—top down, wind in your hair, hard cornering! Whoopee!
- Look good to myself—my first two cars were MG's; I've also had two Triumphs—I love roadsters!
- Spend less money—less than a BMW Z-car, a Porsche Boxster, or other similar cars.
- Play more—now driving to work becomes play, not one more chore.
- Save more money—less expenditure on repairs because the car is more dependable.

The S2000 doubtless has hundreds of features—I haven't driven one yet, so I don't know all the details. Even so, specific features that would likely come up in any demonstration or test drive include: performance measures (speed, cornering, stopping distance), convenience features (automatic convertible top, GPS navigation system), luxury accessories (sound system, leather seats), safety features (air-bags, ABS), and reliability data (it's a Honda, for heaven's sake).

Remember, though, all of these are *features*, and customers buy *benefits*. Let's take a look at how we bridge from features to benefits, so we are sure we are talking about issues that solve the customer's problem.

Learning to "Bridge"

Remember our old aphorism from chapter 6 on Discovery? We spent all that time in chapter 6 talking about how to question and listen because—as we've said before:

> *"If you listen long enough, people will tell you how to sell them!"*

That is, people will tell you what matters to them, they will tell you the problem that drove them into the market, and they will tell you the purchase criteria they are looking for in the solution they seek. If we can solve the problem and provide a solution that meets all (or even most) of the purchase criteria, we get the business.

Bridging is an important skill in helping prospective customers understand how your solution fits their purchase criteria to solve their problem. Bridging is a useful antidote to our very human tendency to assume that a customer will automatically understand how a feature of our program, product, or service meets their needs and solves their problem(s).

In my experience selling, this is a fallacious assumption. That is, customers often miss an important benefit that matters to them. Customers regularly hear a feature, yet never take themselves to the core benefit that matters most in solving the problem they brought to the market in the first place.

For instance, let's assume for a moment that our product comes with a one-year, no-hassle return policy and—just to make it easy—also costs ten percent less than our competitor's product. These are both *good things*, but neither of them is a benefit to the customer.

In the current state, both of these product features are unsupported assertions. We have said it but—from the customer's viewpoint—that doesn't make it so! Lots of stuff gets said in sales interactions that has no basis in truth.

How in the world do we bridge from an unsupported assertion to the detailed benefits that will solve the prospective customer's problems and make the sale for us?

Proving the Feature

We begin with support—the underlying facts or data that prove the feature. Anybody can say anything in a sales situation—in fact, they often do! It is detailed support that makes the feature real to the customer. Support is the key first step in concretizing and proving a feature so we can then bridge from the feature to the ultimate benefit.

In the example above, we can easily prove the return policy with a document stating—in clear, simple, non-legalese—the basics of the return policy. This proves the return policy is real and not just some heat-of-the-moment, smoke-and-mirrors part of the sales spiel. The return policy is still a feature—we have not yet made it a benefit—but it is now a feature with concrete support, not simply an unsupported assertion.

Let's reflect now on price—we have said that our product is priced ten percent lower than the competition. How do we support this assertion? Supporting a price feature requires two things—a written price offering for our product, and written prices for the other competitors who are in the hunt for this sale. Once we have both of those items, we can prove the feature. Remember: even after we have all this information, price is still not a benefit. But at least it is now a feature with black-and-white support.

Making the Bridge

Fine. We've got these two features and they now both have tangible support. We can prove that we have a one-year, no-hassle return policy, and we can also prove that we are priced ten percent below our competitors. What next?

Now we bridge. We take the customer's hand and walk him or her (metaphorically at least) from the feature, across the chasm of doubt to the benefit that addresses their problem. And we begin by reviewing the Universal Benefit List found in Figure 7-2.

In fact, let's do this as an exercise. Look back at Figure 7-2 and identify all the universal benefits that could accrue from having a one-year, no-hassle return policy for your product. List those benefits below—you should be able to identify at least three without having to break your head too much.

1. ______________________________
2. ______________________________
3. ______________________________
4. ______________________________
5. ______________________________

Now look once again at the list in Figure 7-2 and identify all the Universal Benefits that could apply to a purchase where our product is priced ten percent below the competitors. Again, you should be able to identify at least three—list them below.

1. ______________________________
2. ______________________________
3. ______________________________
4. ______________________________
5. ______________________________

Okay—what did you come up with? The way I read it, the one-year no-hassle return policy could reasonably be said to generate each of these benefits for the customer:

- Have fewer hassles
- Look good to others/get recognition/be a hero
- Look good to myself
- Be secure (if the product doesn't work, I'm covered)
- Spend less money (if the product breaks down, I can return it)
- Avoid pain (the psychological pain or regular breakdowns count)

How many of these did you have? Do you see why the policy itself is just a piece of paper? What the customer is really buying is the benefits that accrue from the feature (the return policy)—things like the benefits listed above.

Now let's look at the Universal Benefits that accrue from the ten-percent lower price guarantee:

- Spend less money
- Save more money
- Look good to others/get recognition/be a hero
- Look good to myself
- Avoid pain (the psychological pain of paying too much certainly counts as pain)

Our job is to take our customers and help them bridge from the features we enumerate to the benefits that solve their problem. We do that by in a three-step process:

1. Name the feature on which you are focusing,
2. Support the feature with relevant facts and data, and
3. Bridge to the Universal Benefit by walking the customer over the chasm of doubt to the Universal Benefit(s) that address(es) the problem they are trying to solve.

Let me give you an example. Remember the Honda S2000 we discussed several pages back? Let's take a look at how a professional salesperson might talk with me about Honda's legendary dependability and the benefit to me. We'll use the three-step model above: Name-Support-Bridge as we work on the example. Here's how it might look:

Name the Feature: "*You've mentioned that dependability is an important attribute for you and—having owned several British sports cars myself—I can see why this is so critical for you. As you know, Honda vehicles regularly rank among the most dependable vehicles on the road.*" (This is a very good job of naming the feature, although so far the feature is just an unsupported assertion. Now on to Step 2.)

Support the Feature: *"Here are the most recent J.D. Power initial quality rankings—you'll see the Honda product line leads the pack. And this recent Consumer Reports article speaks to the quality and durability of the S2000 model itself.* (This is a good job of support, but the salesperson hasn't yet bridged to the benefits that will accrue from these features. Let's see how that goes in the last step.)

Bridge to the Benefit: *"What all these data mean to you is that you can buy the S2000 with the assurance that dependability won't be an issue. You can be confident in your choice—selecting the S2000 gives you Honda's legendary dependability with the speed and performance of a fine roadster. But you don't have the hassles of trying to maintain a temperamental European-made automobile. It's the best of both worlds—as fun as a Beemer or Benz without the maintenance costs or breakdown hassles. Plus it costs less on the front end, so you save money there as well..*

And there you have it. In three simple steps (name-support-bridge) we have spoken to one of the customer's problems and moved closer to the sale. All is well and good, but how will you do it for the product you sell? Let's take a look.

Making It Real I: What Are the Features of Your Product?

My guess is that you are not selling fire extinguishers, parachutes, or even life insurance. While these products proved useful for illustration, you make your living selling something altogether different. And your product has a far different feature profile than any of the products we have discussed thus far. So let's "play with real money"—let's talk about the product that makes *your* living, the product that feeds your family, and pays your mortgage. Let's look at the features *you* deal with everyday.

I'm going to walk you through a quick exercise to help you identify the features of your product. You don't even have to think about benefits yet—let's just talk about the features. As we do this exercise, we will be filling out the chart below.

Instructions: Figure 7-3 is designed to help you fully understand the notion of features and benefits as they apply to the product you sell. Complete the chart by column: that is, go down each column and complete it fully before you move to the next column.

1. Begin by listing—in Column 1—the six most important features of the product you sell. The features should be easy to identify—just pull them from the list of all the features you had to memorize when you began selling. Refer back to the beginning of the chapter if you need to—this column is the place to list specs, warranties, applications, quality claims, and so forth.

2. Then identify—in Column 2—the support you have for each feature. That is, how can you prove that the assertion made by the feature is true? Do you have data from an independent rating agency? Do you have test results? How would a skeptical buyer (caveat emptor) know that you are telling the truth when you present the feature you have detailed in Column 1?

3. Finally—in Column 3—detail why the feature should matter to your typical customer. What is it about this feature that applies to the customer's situation?

Charting My Product's Features

	Feature	Support for Feature*	Why it Matters to the Customer**
1.			
2.			
3.			
4.			
5.			
6.			

* A feature with no support is called an unsupported assertion and is not worth a bucket of warm spit in the selling world.

** If it doesn't matter to the customer, it doesn't matter, period. So don't talk about it, already.

Figure 7-3

Making It Real II: What Benefits Are Associated with the Features You Have Identified?

It's not enough to know the features that characterize your product. Salespeople always want to talk about features, while customers only buy benefits. And customers buy the benefits that solve the problem they walked in the door with in the first place. (The problem we should have fully identified in the discovery section of the selling process.) So what benefits are associated with the features you identified in Figure 7-3? Review the discussion about the Universal Benefits found on page 148 and then complete the exercise below.

Instructions: Figure 7-4 is designed to help you wrap your mind around the benefits (the reasons to care) for your customer associated with the product features you have just identified. Again, complete Figure 7-4 by column: that is, go down each column and complete it fully before you move to the next column.

Begin by again listing—in Column 1—the six most important features (you may want to refer to Figure 7-3) of the product you sell. Then identify—in Column 2—up to three benefits associated with each feature you have noted. Finally—in Column 3—detail why the feature should matter to your typical customer. What is it about *this* feature that applies to *this* customer's situation?

Identifying the Benefits That Derive from Each Feature

	Feature	Benefit Accruing from Feature*	Why Benefit Solves Customer Problem**
1.		•	
		•	
		•	
2.		•	
		•	
		•	
3.		•	
		•	
		•	
4.		•	
		•	
		•	
5.		•	
		•	
		•	
6.		•	
		•	
		•	

* A feature with no associated benefit for this customer is a waste of time. Don't talk about it.

** If it doesn't matter to this customer, it doesn't matter, period.

Figure 7-4

Making It Real III: How Do You Bridge from the Features You Have Memorized to the Benefits the Buyers Care About?

In the next chapter we are going to explore how to make the case for your product. That is, we will examine how to present your program, product, or service as the solution to whatever problem first brought your customer into the market. But before we move on to making the case, there's one more skill you need to learn.

A key component of making the case is the ability to bridge from a feature of your product to the associated benefit—the reason to care that helps solve the customer's problem. In every case, you are bridging from the particular feature to one of the universal benefits we reviewed in Figure 7-1 on page 138.

The question we are answering for the customer is WSIGAF? —Why should I give a flip about this feature? How does this feature provide a benefit that solves the problem that brought me into the marketplace?

We will briefly discuss two ways of bridging: 1) beginning with the feature and moving to the benefit/problem solution or 2) beginning with the problem solution/benefit and backing into the feature that addresses these issues. Either method is effective; I suggest you use both for variety and to avoid repetition.

In the exercise below, the hard work has already been done for you. For each of the six examples, complete it in a way that a customer would understand how the feature provided a benefit that solved a problem the customer had.

Remember at the beginning of the chapter when I said that this material is hard and you have to pay attention to get it right? Well this is the hardest part. This is the place most salespeople go into the ditch most often.

Focus here, while I give you some examples. Each of these examples comes from the illustrations we used earlier in the chapter: fire extinguishers, parachutes, and life insurance policies. They each approach the task of bridging from a slightly different angle, but they all achieve the same result—they bridge from the feature to the benefit that solves the customer's problem.

In each case you will see some variation of a model that looks like this:

1. Remind the Customer of the Problem that brought them into the market in the first place. *"You mentioned that XYZ was a major concern for you."*

2. State the Relevant Feature that will solve their problem. *"This product has (state feature or features that address the problem)...."*

3. Use a Bridge Phrase that will lead the customer from the feature of your product to the benefit that solves their problem. *"What this means to you is..."*

4. Lay the Benefit out in plain view so the customer will not have to leap to the benefit on their own. This means that you finish the sentence begun in Step 3. *"What this means to you is that you will have fewer hassles/save more money/etc."*

5. Support the Benefit so that it is not an unsupported assertion. *"I have (provide examples) that prove this is not just my opinion, it's a fact!"*

Bridging Features to Benefits—Examples

Fire Extinguishers: "You mentioned that saving money was one of your key objectives(1). (There's the problem *and* the purchase criteria!) Unlike many extinguishers at this economical price point(2), this fire extinguisher can be recharged(2) when it is used or has expired." (Two features: low price point and recharge-ability.) "What this means to you is(3) that you will save money(4) on the initial investment because of the lower price(5), and you will save money(4) in the long run because it is cheaper to recharge fire extinguishers than to replace them(5)."

1. Remind them of the problem
2. State the relevant features
3. Use a bridge phrase
4. Lay the benefit out in plain view
5. Support the benefit

Parachutes: "This parachute has the latest technology in a steerable canopy(1). Now that you have graduated to competition diving, pinpoint accuracy is more than a hope or a dream, it's a performance demand(2). This highly maneuverable canopy will allow you to hit the target dead-on(3), and increase your chances of winning every time you jump(4)."

1. State the relevant feature
2. Remind them of the problem
3. Tell them what the feature means to them
4. Lay the benefit out in plain view

Life Insurance: You mentioned your need to provide a lot of security(1) for your young family, while keeping your financial outlay to a minimum(1). This policy will provide you with $500,000(2) of level-term(2), guaranteed renewable (2) protection(2) from a top-rated insurance company(2). What this means to you(3) is that you can protect those you love for the future(4), and still have enough free cash to enjoy life with them now(4).

1. Remind them of the problem(s)
2. State the relevant features
3. Use a bridge phrase
4. Lay the benefit(s) out in plain view

Instructions: Okay, now it's your turn! Figure 7-5 is designed to help you practice bridging from the features you memorized to the benefits that solve customer problems. Remember, customers buy to solve a problem:

No Problem = No Sale. No Solution = No Sale.

Refer back to figures 7-3 and 7-4. Then, for each of the features you identified, practice bridging to the benefit/problem solution that matters most to the buyer. Each of the examples above has small type answers in the blanks provided—write over them to yield answers that prove you know how to bridge from features to benefits.

Bridging from Features to Benefits: Solving the Customer's Problem

For Feature 1: One feature of this product is ______(state feature)______. This feature yields ______(state benefit)______, which can be especially helpful in helping you address ______(state problem)______.

For Feature 2: You mentioned that you have been having a problem with ______(state problem)______, and that you were particularly interested in ______(state benefit)______.

This product has______(state feature)______, which will deliver the ______(state benefit)______ you were interested in, and help you address ______(state problem)______.

For Feature 3: You mentioned that you have been having a problem with ______(state problem)______. This product has ______(state feature)______, which will deliver the ______(state benefit)______ you were interested in, and help you address ______(state problem)______.

For Feature 4: One feature of this product is ______(state feature)______. What this means to you is ______(state benefit)______, which can be especially helpful in helping you address ______(state problem)______.

For Feature 5: You mentioned that you have been having a problem with ______(state problem)______. This product has ______(state feature)______, which will deliver the ______(state benefit)______ you were interested in, and help you address ______(state problem)______.

For Feature 6: You mentioned that ______(state benefit)______ is especially important to you. We can offer you ______(restate benefit)______ because our product/program/service has ______(state feature)______. And this ______(restate feature)______ will yield ______(restate benefit)______, which will help you solve ______(state problem)______ that you say is so important to you .

Figure 7-5

Features and Benefits—The Wrap-Up

Are you beginning to get it? And are you beginning to see how often—and how *badly*—most salespeople fail when trying to talk about their products? Perhaps you are even seeing some ways you could improve your sales approach—ways you can answer the WSIGAF query with language that matters to the customer.

The features and benefits step is the one, single place where most sales jump the track. If the you haven't questioned well in Discovery, that shortcoming becomes apparent at the Features and Benefits step. And—even if you have questioned well—the sales process can get off-track if you don't bridge effectively from the product attributes (features) you have memorized to the benefits that solve the customer's problem.

Stay in this chapter till you are certain you know the difference between features and benefits, and until you can identify at least one of the Universal Benefits associated with every feature of your product. This investment in preparation will yield enormous dividends for you as you move further into the sales process.

Getting Down to Cases: A Quick Content Review

1. What is a feature? When we talk about features, on what or whom are we focusing? ____________________

   ____

   ____

2. What is a benefit? When we talk about benefits, on what or whom are we focusing? ______________________

____

____

3. What does WSIGAF stand for? How can WSIGAF remind us of an important focus in presenting features and benefits? ______________________________

____

____

4. How many Universal Benefits are there? Which ones (circle them on page 148) do you think are most applicable to your product or service? ____________

____

____

5. To what does the word "bridging" apply? How might you use this in your sales presentations? ____________

____

____

6. Have you ever made an "unsupported assertion"? How did it work out for you? What might you do to support the assertion so that you are more credible in your sales presentations? ______________________

____

____

Key Reminders

- People buy to solve a problem—real or perceived.
  No solution = No sale
- Customers buy the benefits that solve the problem they walked in the door with in the first place.
- A *feature* is an attribute of a product, program, or service.
- A *benefit* is a reason for the customer to care (and to buy).
- Salespeople are tempted to talk about *features,* while customers focus on *benefits.*
- There are fewer than fifty benefits in the world. These benefits—the Universal Benefits—drive every sale ever made.
- The Universal Benefits relate to money, power, prestige, self-understanding, fear, and the other core motivators that drive human behavior.
- Features need to be translated into benefits—walk the prospect across the bridge! (In answering the questions, always bridge from the feature to the associated benefit.)

8
Presenting the Solution

You have likely heard the familiar phrase "When you are up to your ass in alligators, it is hard to remember that your initial objective was to drain the swamp!" It's so true—in the fray of the moment, whatever "the moment" is—it's often easy to lose sight of our overall objective.

Likewise in selling. We get totally absorbed in the mechanics of making a good first impression, asking appropriate questions, and listening carefully to the responses customers give us. We busy ourselves with professionally presenting our product's features, then carefully bridging those features to benefits that matter to the customer. And—in all this—we lose sight of the overall objective: to fully address the problem or problems that brought the customer to the sales interaction in the first place, and to make the case that *our* solution is the *best* solution for the customer.

Where Is Making the Case in the Sales Process?

Early in our work together (chapter 3—The Sales Process), we talked about having to earn the right to move to the next step in the sales process. By the time we get to the point of Making the Case (Step 5 in the sales process) for our product, program, or service, we have invested a great deal of time and energy in the customer and in the process of solving the customer's problem.

We have *earned the right to make the case for our solution* by meeting the prospective customer in a professional way, and connecting with her or him in a manner that builds rapport. We have listened well in discovery, and have helped the buyer refine his or her understanding of the problem he or she seeks to solve.

And we have carefully presented our features to the customer—talking only about the ones that matter to him or her, and always remembering to bridge to the benefits that derive from each feature we identify. By following this process professionally—and responding to the customer's needs—we've *earned the right to present a solution* to the problem that drove the customer into the market in the first place.

The highlighted box in Figure 8-1 pinpoints exactly where we are in the sales process. You'll see that—in making the case—we are now at Step 5, well on our way to completing the sale. As we begin making the case, we are taking everything we have learned in Steps 1 through 4 and we are weaving it all into a powerful statement that says: "You will solve your problem when you buy from me!" Take a look:

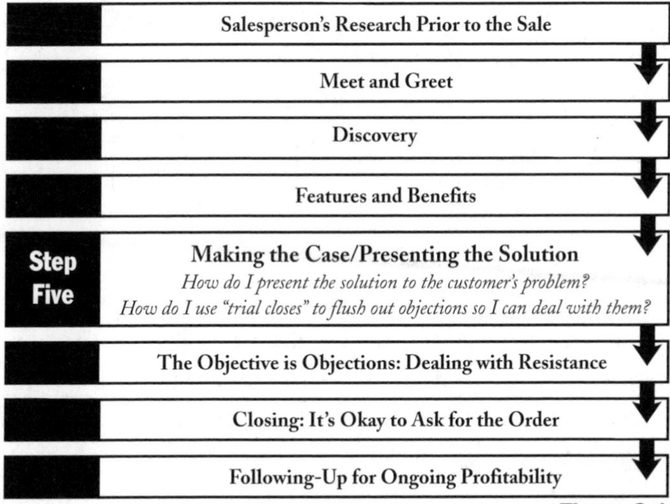

Salesperson's Research Prior to the Sale
Meet and Greet
Discovery
Features and Benefits
Step Five
Making the Case/Presenting the Solution
How do I present the solution to the customer's problem?
How do I use "trial closes" to flush out objections so I can deal with them?
The Objective is Objections: Dealing with Resistance
Closing: It's Okay to Ask for the Order
Following-Up for Ongoing Profitability

Figure 8-1

While Figure 8-1 tells us exactly where we are in the selling process, there is additional critical information we need before we can fully make the case for buying from us. We need to know how fully the customer is aware of his or her problem—and the Problem-Awareness Grid helps us determine that key information.

The Problem-Awareness Grid

We have said many times that customers buy to solve a problem—real or perceived. The key to knowing how to proceed when making the case in a sales presentation is to fully understand where the customer is on the Problem-Awareness Grid (Figure 8-2). Take a look at the grid and we'll walk through what it can teach us.

Figure 8-2 is a simple two-by-two matrix. The vertical columns assess whether a customer actually has a problem —with the left column saying, "Yes, there is a problem" and the right column saying "No, there is not a problem".

The horizontal rows gauge the prospective customer's awareness of the problem. In the top row the customer's response is, "Yes, I'm aware of the situation;" in the lower row the customer's response is, "No, I'm not aware of the situation."

As the rows and the columns intersect, we wind up with four distinct quadrants; you'll find them numbered as Quadrants 1 to 4 in Figure 8-2. Take a hard look at the Figure 8-2, then we'll see how all this applies to the world of making a sale.

Make sure you understand how the columns and the rows intersect, and also that you understand the worldview of a customer in each of the four quadrants. As an example, a customer in Quadrant 1 has a problem (from the vertical column heading) and knows he or she has a problem (from the horizontal row heading). We'll explore all this in much more detail shortly.

The Problem-Awareness Grid

Prospect ***has a problem and knows it.*** 1	2 *Prospect* ***has no problem*** *and* ***knows s/he has no problem.***
3 *Prospect* ***has a problem,*** *but is* ***not aware*** *that he/she has no problem.*	4 *Prospect* ***has no problem,*** *but is* ***not aware*** *of the problem.*

Figure 8-2

Figure 8-3 (page 176) is the beginning of applying what we observed above to the sales process we have been using throughout our work together. Examine Figure 8-3 closely—it is critical to understand this information if you are to fully satisfy your prospective customers, and develop long-term relationships with those prospects you can't sell today.

As in Figure 8-2, Figure 8-3 presents four quadrants made from the intersection of the vertical columns and the horizontal rows above. Figure 8-3, however, fleshes out our understanding by including text in each of the four quadrants. Let's review each quadrant briefly—taking a look at the situation of a typical buyer who might occupy each quadrant—then we'll examine the figure itself.

Quadrant 1

Customers who find themselves in Quadrant 1 are those who have a problem *and* know they have a problem. These are the easiest customers to deal with; you'll see why in a moment. It is not uncommon for customers to be aware of part of their problem but not all of it. In that case, a customer would be in Quadrant 1, as well as in Quadrant 3. (See below)

Quadrant 2

Customers in Quadrant 2 are those who don't have a problem *and* know they don't have a problem. This customer rarely calls you or walks into your place of business—that would be wasting your time and their own, which is not their style. The most common way to meet these folks is when you are handed a list of prospects to cold call, or when you begin canvassing an industry group.

Selling to these folks might seem hopeless, but it isn't. We'll talk about how to build bridges to this group in just a few moments.

Quadrant 3

Prospective customers in Quadrant 3 have a problem, *but* they are not yet aware of their problem. Perhaps they are buying from a supplier who is overcharging them. Or they may be buying the same product they bought three years ago—unaware that new (and far better) options are now available to them. There is a problem there to solve, if we can only bring it to the customer's awareness and get the customer to acknowledge it.

Remember—just because someone thinks he or she does not have a problem does not mean they are right. You can, by careful questioning, help uncover a problem the buyer did not know existed, and then be able to move them from Quadrant 3 to Quadrant 1.

Quadrant 4

Buyers who occupy Quadrant 4 fall into one of two distinct groups: 1) the worrywarts or, 2) the clueless. In both cases, Quadrant 4 represents those who have no problem, *but* don't know they have no problem.

That is, the worrywarts *think* they may have a problem—but it's only a hunch. They have no data. The oblivious are pretty sure they don't have a problem, but they don't really know, either, because they don't have any data—and don't know they need data!

In both cases, our job is to give the customers data—even if it's only perceptual data—and move them from Quadrant 4 to Quadrant 1 so we can sell them in a straight-on sale. We'll see how to do that in just a moment.

Take a hard look at Figure 8-3, and make sure you know what each quadrant represents and the worldview of customers in each quadrant.

The Problem-Awareness Grid
Adding Some Meat to the Bones

Prospect ***has a problem and knows it.*** 1	2 *Prospect* ***has <u>no</u> problem*** *and* ***knows s/he has no problem.***
3 *Prospect* ***has a problem,*** *but is* ***not aware*** *that he/she has no problem.*	4 *Prospect* ***has no problem,*** *but is* ***not aware*** *of the problem.*

Figure 8-3

Using the Problem-Awareness Grid to Make the Sale

Since each of the four quadrants in our Problem-Awareness Grid represents a different situation for the prospective customer, each quadrant calls for a different strategy in making the sale. We want to do the same thing in making the case/presenting the solution that we did in presenting features and benefits to the customer. That is, we want to custom-tailor our presentation to the unique needs, perceptions, and circumstances of the customer with whom we are dealing.

This custom-tailoring includes keeping the customer's level of problem-awareness at the top of our minds as we are present our solution/make our case. Let's take a look at how that might play out for each of our four quadrants.

Refer to Figure 8-4 as we walk through the sales response appropriate for each of the four quadrants.

The Problem-Awareness Grid
***Salesperson Responses* for Each Quadrant**

Prospect ***has a problem and knows it.*** *Negotiate (and solve)* 1	*Prospect* ***has <u>no</u> problem*** *and* ***knows s/he has no problem.*** *Wait (and build relationship)* 2
3 *Prospect* ***has a problem,*** *but is* ***not aware*** *that he/she has no problem.* *Educate (raise awareness)*	4 *Prospect* ***has no problem,*** *but is* ***not aware*** *of the problem.* *Agitate (create doubt)*

Figure 8-4

Quadrant 1—Customer has a problem and knows he has a problem

Most prospective customers will be in Quadrant 1 when you encounter them—they will have a problem, and they will know they have a problem. In this simplest of sales situations, all we need do—as shown in Figure 8-4, Quadrant 1 —is negotiate on the terms and definition of the problem, then solve the problem in a way that satisfies the customer.

This is not to minimize the work involved in selling a Quadrant 1 customer. We still have to question well and listen carefully, we still have to match features and benefits to the specifics of the customer's situation, and we still have to *bridge the features* to benefits that matter to the customer.

It's still hard work, but at least we are starting from common ground: the customer has a problem, the customer knows s/he has a problem, and the customer has invited us into the process of solving the problem. That's a heck of basis on which to build a sales relationship! And from that point it is not terribly complex to negotiate on the terms and understanding of the problem, then to solve the problem in a way that helps both the buyer and the salesperson reach a good outcome.

Most sales training points towards the scenario in Quadrant 1, and this book is no exception. Still—to make all the sales we can possibly make—we must know how to sell the other three quadrants as well. So let's take a look…

Quadrant 2—Customer has no problem and knows he has no problem

I refer to folks in Quadrant 2 as *savvy consumers.* They keep up with markets and they know what is available. They regularly evaluate their suppliers, and *they know what kind of service they are getting*. And they know it when they don't have a problem.

As an example, consider a moderate-sized investor who has his entire portfolio with a single investment advisor. The investor and the advisor meet quarterly to review goals, portfolio mix, and portfolio performance against the S&P

and other relevant indices. In addition, the investor and the advisor are friends—they attend the same church, and play tennis together periodically.

This savvy investor does not have a problem. And he knows it. Brokers cold calling this guy from some boiler-room are out of luck: no problem=no sale. Even other friends who happen to be brokers are out of luck. This relationship works.

So do we just throw up our hands when we encounter a prospect like this? Not necessarily. It all depends on the relative value of the prospect, and on how much time we have to wait. Waiting is the key to dealing with customers of this type.

Take a look at Figure 8-4, Quadrant 2. How do we deal with the savvy customer—the one who doesn't have a problem and knows he doesn't have a problem? We build a relationship. And we wait. Sooner or later the current supplier will stumble. And when he does, we will be in a position to pounce. But only if we have an existing relationship when the stumble occurs.

You have, as a buyer, perhaps experienced someone trying to sell you when you were in Quadrant 2. A salesperson approaches you and your rebuff them with the response that you are "not interested." (That is—you don't have a problem and you know you don't have a problem.)

The salesperson replies: *"I can understand that. Would you mind if I call you back in a couple of months to see if your needs have changed?"* You assent to the callback just to get the salesperson off the phone, and don't think anything else about it.

Lo and behold, he or she actually does call you back in sixty days! You are astounded (this person actually does what he or she says he or she will do!) but again you do not buy. The process continues for several cycles, and all the while you defer the purchase, but celebrate the salesperson's professionalism and tenacity. The salesperson is *waiting*—and in the waiting he or she is also beginning to *build a relationship*. When your circumstances change, this person will likely get to pitch the business.

Wait—and build a relationship. That's how you deal with customers in Quadrant 2.

Quadrant 3—Customer has a problem, but does not know he has a problem.

Folks in Quadrant 3 are fun to sell, because we really are doing them a service when we call on them. We are raising to their awareness a problem they have but that they did not know existed. And in doing this, we are helping them solve their problem, and do a better job for themselves and/or for their employer.

Let's pick up on the example from several pages ago. Let's say you have been leasing a piece of equipment (a photocopier, for instance) from a supplier for years. The equipment has worked fine, the price seems fair, you get good service. As far as you are concerned, you do not have a problem. But you may be wrong about that…

Suppose your supplier has new equipment—equipment that could cut your per-copy cost in half. But he has not gotten around to presenting you with this new option. You are not screaming, so *he* doesn't have a problem. And you don't know any better, so you don't *know* you have a problem. But there's a Joker in this deck. And the Joker is about to get dealt.

An office equipment sales rep cold-calls you on the phone and just happens—miracle of miracles—to get through to you. He has to be quick, so his first discovery question is this: "How would you like to save 50 percent on your photocopy equipment and supplies?" You're no dumbass—you listen to his spiel. And, before it's all over, you have moved to Quadrant 1 (has a problem and knows it) and are well on your way to switching suppliers.

Why did this work so well? Because the sales representative helped you realize that you had a problem you had never noticed. He, as Figure 8-4 says, educated you—he raised the problem to your awareness.

One final thing: how are you going to feel toward your old supplier when he next calls on you? This guy had a better deal and didn't give it to you, even though you were a good customer of long-standing. He was probably making better deals with his new accounts than he was with you, even though you had kept him in business for years. You are going to be mad—and rightly so. The key takeaway from this little episode: *look after the customers you've already got*!

How do we help raise problem awareness for Quadrant 3 customers? It's simple, really. A buyer winds up in Quadrant 3 because he or she can't devote as much time to your product category as you can. New options come on the market, alternate ways to reduce costs become available. Most customers can't track this day-to-day. They remain happy—and unaware of their problem—because the solution they have *was a good one when they made it!*

Our job as salespeople is to raise to awareness the new options available—ones that will allow them to do things better, faster, cheaper, and more efficiently than they ever thought possible. The minute the customer becomes aware of a problem, he moves to Quadrant 1 (has a problem and knows it) and we sell by negotiating and solving.

Quadrant 4—Customer has no problem, but does not know he has no problem

As we noted above, the folks in Quadrant 4 represent two very dissimilar groups: the worrywarts and the clueless. In each case, these are people who have no actual problem, but are uncertain about their situation. Interestingly, you sell both subsets of Quadrant 4 in exactly the same way: you agitate and raise doubt about the product, program, or service they are currently buying.

I am *not* arguing here for creating a need where there is no need. What I *am* saying is that there are many different ways to make the case for the products we represent. And two of the most effective ways to talk about our products include: 1) as an answer to a concern held by a worrywart, or 2) as a remedy to an issue you have raised (by agitating) with a clueless buyer. An example might be helpful.

Let's begin with the worrywart. Many years ago I sold in the automotive aftermarket—that is, I sold a product that car owners and mechanics bought *after* the car had been in use for some time. In my case, the product was automobile batteries. My sale was not directly to the mechanic or the consumer—I sold to the warehouses (called WDs—warehouse distributors) that serviced the mechanics and auto parts stores.

Our products were, frankly, of higher quality than the products of most of our competitors. Still, we were a relatively small player in a market dominated by several very large companies. One concern we had to meet and overcome was the "who are you guys?" question. And we were able to meet and overcome this concern by raising other, even more important issues among our prospects in Quadrant 4. We made sales by *agitating*.

As you can imagine, car owners will not wait when they need a new battery. If one mechanic can't get a battery, the car owner just calls a second mechanic or another service station. To be out of stock is invariably to lose the sale.

And this is where I was able to plant seeds of doubt among my prospective customers, and then water those seeds of doubt until they yielded a sale.

"You haven't had any problems with product availability, have you?" I'd query. "They haven't been short-shipping you or stocking-out of some items?" If the customer replied "yes" to either of these questions, that put them up in Quadrant 1 —the easiest quadrant to sell. I solved the problem and asked for the sale.

If the prospective customer indicated he or she had no problems of either type, I'd congratulate them on their good fortune, and mention that *I had heard rumors in the market about some customers having supply problems.* That's agitating and planting seeds of doubt. When problems arose (as they do in all supplier-client relationships) then the problems confirm the suspicions you have planted, and you are there to solve the problem and make the sale.

To reiterate, I *am not* advocating for lying or being disingenuous. I *am* saying that all buyer-supplier relationships are fraught with peril and will eventually have difficulties. If you believe in your product and the organization that represent, then it makes good sense for you to advocate for your prospect to do business with *you*. Actually, the prospect does have one problem, if no other—they are not doing business with you. And you can advocate for them in a way no other salesperson would. So raise this problem, then solve it to make the sale.

How the Problem-Awareness Grid Helps You

Okay, fine, we now have a Problem-Awareness Grid. How in the world does this help me make a sale?

I have done a fair amount of camping in my life, including backcountry camping where a compass and a topographical map are the primary means of navigation. The very first thing you do when using a map in the wilderness is to orient it—to figure out exactly where you are in space, and then to locate that point on the map. *Only when you know precisely where you are can you plot a path to successfully reach your goal.*

The Problem-Awareness Grid is very much like a topographical map for a sales call. With the grid—and with careful questioning and listening—you can determine where the customer is both in terms of *having a problem*, and *knowing he or she has a problem*. And once you know these two things, the grid tells you exactly how to proceed in making the sale.

Using the Problem-Awareness Grid in the Moment

Because this whole way of looking at a prospective customer's situation is brand new to you, it may seem hopelessly complex right now. Do not be dismayed. Look back at our first Problem-Awareness Grid—Figure 8-2 on page 173. Remember, we are only exploring two questions here:

1. Does the prospective customer have a problem—real or perceived?
2. Is the prospective customer aware of his or her problem/situation?

If you know the answer to these two questions, you can use the grid to orient yourself and you know what to do next:

- If the prospective customer has a problem and knows it, then that's Quadrant 1. Solve the problem, negotiate favorable terms, and you've got a sale.
- If the prospective customer has a problem and doesn't yet know it, that's Quadrant 3. Your task is to raise the problem to awareness by educating the customer. Then you solve the problem, negotiate favorable terms, and you've got a sale. The key to making the sale is knowing where you are so you know where you need to go.
- If the prospective customer doesn't have a problem and knows he or she doesn't have a problem, that's Quadrant 2. The challenge here is to build a relationship with the prospect and wait. The current supplier will inevitably stumble —it always happens. When it does, this prospect will move to Quadrant 1 (has a problem and knows it.) And then you can solve the problem and negotiate favorable terms to make yet another sale.
- If the prospective customer doesn't have a problem but is unsure whether he or she has a problem, that is Quadrant 4. The challenge here is to agitate and raise doubt until the prospective customer begins to think he or she has a problem. When this happens, the prospect will move to Quadrant 1 (has a problem and knows it). Then you can solve the problem and negotiate favorable terms to make yet another sale.

David Campbell—once the president of the Center for Creative Leadership—wrote a brief book on leadership entitled *If You Don't Know Where You're Going, You'll Probably Wind Up Somewhere Else*. He's right, of course. We have to know where we are going to be able to achieve our destination. The beauty of the Problem-Awareness Grid is that it not only tells us where we are (Quadrants 1–4, depending on the prospect's situation,) it also tells us what to do next (educate, agitate, negotiate, etc.) to wind up at our destination (an ethical sale to this customer).

People buy to solve a problem—real or perceived. Once we have fully assessed a customer's problem (remember: no problem = no sale), the next step is to use the problem as a launching pad to make the case that we can fully solve the customer's problem.

How to Leverage a Customer's Problem to Make Your Case

The whole of our work with the Problem-Awareness Grid is built on the assumption that we cannot sell prospective customers unless they have a problem—and they know that they have a problem. As we question prospective customers, the problems that come to the surface are often shortcomings of competitive products, or of competitive suppliers. This is a great opportunity for many reasons—not least of which is the customer is already in Quadrant 1: they have a problem and they know it.

Still, it requires some delicacy to pursue these issues without looking like an opportunistic jerk. For some reason, customers have it in their mind that *they* can say all manner of derogatory things about any supplier or product on the market. But if *we* agree with them directly, that's considered bad form—like piling-on or kicking someone who is down.

Still, it makes sense to judiciously use the prospect's irritation with a competitor's product—or with the competitor himself. Here's an easy six-step guide for leveraging the prospective customer's irritation with your competition.

1. Restate the problem as the customer has presented it to you. Although it is considered poor form to bad-mouth your competition, it is considered very good form to *listen closely to potential customers*. Here is where you repeat the frustrations you have heard your customers voice. It might sound something like this: "What I hear you saying is that you have had a lot of problems with (state competitor or competitor's product)."

Beware of putting words in the prospect's mouth at this point—it irritates them mightily. And *make sure you get agreement that you have restated the problem correctly*, because this is the basis for the whole sales presentation. Your quick comment to check for confirmation might sound something like this, "Have I recapped your frustrations correctly? Is there anything I have missed?"

2. Determine the frequency of the problem. Ask the customer how often the issue is arising. A once-in-a-great-while issue is not nearly as frustrating as a problem that occurs repeatedly. Also, the frequency of the problem will help you determine the total impact for the customer, as well as the dollar cost of the problem in the questions that follow.

3. Determine the impact of the problem. Impact is a big category: what does this problem do to your people? To your customers? To morale and enthusiasm in the workplace? Ask pointed questions to make sure the prospective customer fully understands all the ways this issue with the supplier impacts his or her business, employees, and customers.

4. Assign a dollar value to the problem. Impressions are one thing; numbers are quite another. Most purchasers pride themselves on being hard-boiled businesspeople—even if they aren't. So reduce their frustration to a concrete number. If supplier problems are costing them one sale a week, and each sale averages $625.00, then supplier problems are costing them over $32,000 a year. That number will get a prospective customer's attention!

Let's try another one—say a competitor is doing something that makes life harder for his customer. Perhaps the supplier is shipping materials in a jumble, so that the receiving clerk spends ten hours a week straightening things out. Say the receiving clerk makes $10/hour, plus benefits. You can spin this out in one of two ways:

1. "Did you realize that one of your employees is spending a quarter of his work week untangling messes made by this supplier?"

   Or you could say,

2. "If I've done the math right—and you can check me here—you are paying one of your employees $5,200 a year (and this doesn't even include benefits) just to undo messes made by your current supplier!"

What you are trying to do is spin the supplier problem out in a way that makes it look as horrendous as possible. Then offer yourself and your products as the solution as in Steps 5 and 6 below.

5. Recap all you have learned about the scope, impact, and cost of the problem. This is the summary, and it is critical. Summarize everything you have heard about the problem and situation, then get the customer's agreement that you have summarized well. After that you are all set to solve the problem and get the business.

6. Present your product, program, or service as the solution to the problem (and get agreement!) that your solution will solve their problem.

With these guidelines—and by using the Problem-Awareness Grid—you should be well equipped to make the case that your product, program, or service is the best solution to your prospective customer's problems. Read on to discover exactly how to make the case.

Real Salespeople vs. Imposters: The Difference and Why It Matters

In my experience, making the presentation is the sales step that separates the *real* salespeople from the imposters. When *real* salespeople make a sales presentation, they are pulling together everything that has happened in the preceding steps: meet and greet, discovery, features, and benefits—all of 'em. And the *real* salesperson's focus is on earning the customer's business by solving *all* of the customer's problems in the best way possible. Contrast this behavior with that of imposter salespeople…

When imposters make a sales presentation, they are regurgitating a memorized spiel—they are "pitching." Imposters want to sell the customer because selling is their job, not because they have any inherent interest in the customer or his or her problems. Imposter salespeople try to jam the customer's problem into whatever solution-box is available—they are more interested in the sale than in the customer.

It's a shortsighted philosophy, because customers can tell the difference. And they don't like it, either. (Think about your own experience as a customer. Can't you tell when you are being truly listened to, versus when you are just being set-up for a pitch?)

My goal is teach you how to make a sales presentation like the professional you want to be. So you can make the sale, not just make the pitch.

Making the Case: A Simple Six-Step Process

Let's recap briefly: People buy to solve a problem, right? And we have spent the first four steps of the sales process understanding their problem, and earning the right to help them solve it. Our primary task in the early steps was to listen and build credibility; in Step 4 we actually began to talk about the product or service we bring to the market. In the early portions of this chapter we took a hard look at locating our customers on our Problem-Awareness Grid, so we knew how to proceed in relating to them.

But all this hard work was only preamble—we were *earning the right to make our case.* We were earning the right to solve the problem. Now we have done that, and it's time to look at a simple process for making the case that we can solve the customer's problem better than any other competitor. Here's the process; see how it applies to the customers you deal with every day.

A Simple Six-Step Process for Making the Case

1. Restate the problem(s) you and the prospective customer have identified. Be sure to get the prospect to agree to your problem list by asking for additions or amplifications.
2. Deal with each of the problems you have identified in turn, and make the case that your product or service offers the best solution for each of the problems.
3. Always bridge from the features of a your product to the benefits that matter to the customer and solve the customer's problem. Remember: customers don't care about facts per se, but they do care about solving the problem that brought them into the market. Be sure you *speak to the benefits that solve the customer's problems.*
4. As you make the case that you have solved a portion of the customer's problem, repeat back anything you hear the customer saying about your solution. This will ensure that you have heard the customer correctly, and dealt with any concerns he or she might have.
5. Use tie-down questions (see pages 194–195) to ensure that the prospect agrees with each part of the solution as you make your case. The goal is to tie-up all loose ends on one component of the sale before moving on to the next component.
6. Use a trial close (see pages 196–197) to gauge the customer's receptivity to the overall case you have made, and to flush out any objections. (We'll review how to deal with objections in chapter 9.)

This is all there is in making your case. It's far simpler than most people imagine. The key thing to remember—and it's a thread woven throughout the steps above—is to focus on solving the prospective customer's problem. If, after you make the case, the customer does not think you can solve the problem, then you've got a big problem. But if you listen well and fully understand the prospect's circumstances, making the case is as simple as carefully matching product features and benefits to each portion of the customer's problem.

Do I need a piece of rope to ask a tie-down question?

Every time I see the phrase "tie-down question" my mind flashes to rodeo scenes from the American southwest. I imagine a cowboy leaping from a horse to secure the hooves of a steer with a short length of rope. While tie-down questions don't require rope, they serve a similar purpose to the tie used in steer roping. A roped steer is unable to wander off; the rope secures the steer and settles the "wander off" issue once and for all.

Likewise, a tie-down question settles once and for all that the customer's issue has been tied-down. Because you have established that the issue is resolved, the customer is unlikely to wander back to the issue at some later point in the sale.

Tie-down questions are quite simple. The key thing is to remember to use them before you move on in making your case. Here are some tie-down questions I have found useful:

- Do you feel like what we have talked about will solve this portion of the problem?
- How does that sound? Does it deal with the concerns you have raised?
- Do you think this will work? Why? Why not?
- Has that addressed your problem? What questions do you have? Can we move on to the next issue?

Here's how you might use a tie-down question while selling to a new customer. The prospective customer asks you about the reliability of your product—they have had problems with their current product, and this is one of the problems that has taken them into the market. (They are in Quadrant 1—all you need do here is negotiate and solve.)

You do an excellent job of feature-benefiting the reliability dimensions of your product. You detail the features and then you bridge to the associated benefits. You support your features with relevant data to avoid unsupported assertions, then you check to make sure that the customer understands what you have said. And now you're ready for the tie-down question.

You look the customer in the eye and ask, "How does that sound? Have I dealt with your concerns about reliability?" If they answer "yes" you can be pretty sure you have put this issue to bed, and won't have to deal with it again. That's the beauty, in fact, of tie-down questions: they tie-down the customer's agreement with your presentation of a particular feature/benefit and its impact on the customer's problem.

What the heck is a trial close?

In chapter 9 we will deal with trial closes in much more detail than we do here. Still, it's important to have an introduction so you will understand this sixth step in the process we use to make the case.

A trial close is nothing but a tie-down question on steroids. A tie-down question addresses one portion of the case you are making ("Does this solution deal with issue X?"). A trial close, on the other hand, assesses the prospective customer's response to the entire case you have made ("Based on what I have proposed, do you think I have solved the problem and hit your objectives?").

Here are some common trial-close questions—use the ones you most prefer, or create some that better serve your needs.

- What concerns do you have so far?
- Have I dealt with all the issues you brought to our meeting?
- What's left that we haven't addressed?
- How does this sound so far?

The trial close is an important part of making the case, because it helps you know where to go next. If your trial close works (that is, if the customer agrees that you have solved their problem) then you can begin to close the sale and nail down the follow-up. If your trial close flushes out an objection (and this is the most common outcome when you make a trial close) you can probe and deal with the objection, then circle back to a second trial close.

Talking about Price

Price is one of the places we all get hung-up as salespeople. Most of us, most of the time, don't have the lowest price. And we don't want to compete on price anyhow, because *a customer bought with a low price will be lost to the first supplier who comes along with an even lower price.* But it's not like you can ignore price—in the end you are going to have to send invoices, and most rational customers want to know what is going to be on the invoice. So how do we talk about price without looking like a blithering idiot, or hurting our chances to make the sale.

Here are several pointers that I have found useful when talking about price:

1. Don't lead with price. If the price is beyond what the prospect thinks is reasonable, he or she will quit listening the minute you give a price and your chance to make the case is finished.
2. Build value before talking price. A bad deal is a bad deal at most any price. Our first task in making the case is to make sure we have sold our solution to the prospect. Remember: people buy to solve a problem. Sell your solution thoroughly before you hang a price tag on it.

3. Make sure any price comparisons are apples to apples. It's easy to get trapped when a prospective customer says, "But the last guy's price was a third lower than yours!" Here is the place to make sure you are talking about comparable offers. There are many ways to get a lower price. Make sure the two offers are identical in warranty, terms, delivery, quality of product, advertising support, and any other attribute that weighs into sales in your industry.
4. Don't apologize for your price. It is what it is. If it's higher, you don't have to call attention to it. The customer will notice on his or her own. Don't apologize—your product is worth what it costs. If you don't believe it is worth what it costs, then advocate for lower prices or quit. It is impossible to sell a product you don't believe in.
5. Make sure you continually point the customer back to your TVP. The TVP is the Total Value Proposition of the case you make for buying your product. It includes the price of the product, the reputation of the product and of your company as a supplier, the terms and conditions of the sale, and the opportunity to do business with you.

Talking about price is hard because it is a place we often get beat up in the sales world. The price discussion also offers you an opportunity to differentiate yourself from your competitors. You can make the case that you and your solution offer more than just low price—you offer best value. For *most* customers, in *most* product categories, *most* of the time, best value is what they are really after as they seek to solve the problem that drove them into the market in the first place.

If you have done a good job in the sales process, you always have one competitive advantage over other offers: yourself! The only way the customer can work with you is to buy from you. Your job is to be good enough to make him or her want to work with you—even if your price is higher.

Getting Down to Cases: A Quick Content Review and Opportunity to Apply What You Have Learned

We have observed how important it is to make the case well —this is where the whole sales process converges to solve the customer's problem. Answer each of the questions below to test your mastery of the material in chapter 8. You are welcome to review the material in the chapter as you answer the questions, but please take them seriously. You learn the most when you take the chapter material to the challenges you face every day.

1. What steps precede Making the Case in our sales process? Why is the information from those steps critical to making a successful case in Step 5?

2. Review the Problem-Awareness Grid in Figure 8-3. In which quadrant would you place most of the prospective customers you encounter? What is the appropriate strategy to sell customers in this quadrant?

3. Fill in the blanks below.

   Customers don't buy programs or products, they buy

   __________________________.

   No __________________________ = no sale.

4. Briefly capsule the six-step process we use to leverage problems our prospects are having with their current supplier. ______________________________

____

5. What is a trial close? When is it appropriate to use a trial close? Give two examples of trial closes that apply in the sales world where you make your living. ______________

____

____

6. What is a tie-down question? What, exactly, does it tie-down? Give three examples of tie-down questions you could use in the selling you do. ______________

____

____

7. Should you lead with price when making the case? Why or why not? Do you have the lowest price when you go to market with the product or service you sell? ________

____

____

8. What is a TVP? How might it help you in making your case? What is the TVP for the product or service you sell?

____

____

Key Reminders

- Customers don't buy program or products, customers buy solutions.
- No solution = No sale
- The key to knowing how to proceed when solving the problem and making the case is to fully understand where the customer is on the Problem-Awareness Grid.
- Each quadrant in the Problem-Awareness Grid calls for a different strategy to make the sale.
    1. **Quadrant 1** (Has a problem and knows it)—Negotiate/Solve
    2. **Quadrant 2** (Has no problem and knows it)—Wait/Build Relationship
    3. **Quadrant 3** (Has a problem and does not know it)—Educate/Raise Awareness
    4. **Quadrant 4** (Has no problems and does not know it)—Agitate/Create Doubt
- Don't make the pitch, make the case! (The six-step process can show you how!)
- Tie-down questions ensure that you have really settled a particular issue.

- Watch for a buying sign, then move to the trial close!

Five pointers on price:

1. Don't lead with price.
2. Build value before talking price.
3. Make sure any price comparisons are apples to apples.
4. Don't apologize for your price.
5. Make sure you continually point the customer back to your TVP.

9
Dealing with Resistance

Ah! sweet objections. Is there anything in all of selling that strikes more fear into the heart of salespeople? I think not.

Some folks will tell you that rejection is even worse than objections—and rejection is a fearful thing, as well. But rejection is just an objection on steroids; the customer objects so strenuously that the salesperson gets thrown out, either literally or (more likely) figuratively.

Objection is the point in the whole sales process most likely to cause a salesperson to become a blithering idiot. This is the point at which salespeople (me included) hope the floor will open up under them and they will just drop right through—into a blissful land of acquiescent buyers and compliant purchasing agents.

Sadly, such a land does not exist. But there is a cure for objecto-phobia. And we're going to explore it right now.

How Does the Objections Stage Figure into the Overall Sales Process?

Remember, we're working with a disciplined sales process. The sales process we began tracking in chapter 3 is every bit as applicable now as it has been in the past. Customers begin with a problem they are trying to solve (chapter 2). They then move through predictable steps: gathering data, clarifying the need, meeting you, and listening to you present your product or program as the solution to the problem that brought them into the market in the first place. Take a quick look at Figure 9-1 to remind yourself where we are in the sales process, then we'll move forward and explore how to deal with objections. You'll find objections highlighted as Step 6—right after Making the Case. In fact, *making the case often causes objections to surface.*

Figure 9-1 locates objections in our sales process model.

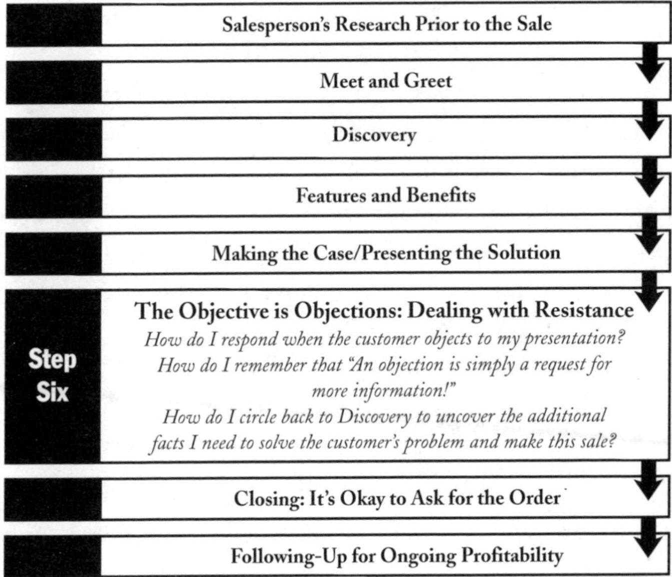

Salesperson's Research Prior to the Sale
Meet and Greet
Discovery
Features and Benefits
Making the Case/Presenting the Solution
Step Six
The Objective is Objections: Dealing with Resistance
How do I respond when the customer objects to my presentation?
How do I remember that "An objection is simply a request for more information!"
How do I circle back to Discovery to uncover the additional facts I need to solve the customer's problem and make this sale?
Closing: It's Okay to Ask for the Order
Following-Up for Ongoing Profitability

Figure 9-1

Objections occur at this point in the process because, as you make your case, you are saying: "You brought me a problem and here is the solution for your problem. I have solved your problem, now buy from me." When you say this, customers often remember components of the problem not-previously identified; these neglected components of the problem become objections.

I do not believe most customers deliberately withhold information just so they can object, though sometimes you'll be tempted to think that. Instead, the process of moving towards a decision causes the prospective customer to reexamine the problem. And objections emerge from this closer scrutiny of the problem.

"Oh My Gosh—They Won't Buy It!"

Objections can occur at any point in the sales process, but the most common place for serious objections to arise is when you reach Step 5 and begin to make the case that you—better than anyone else—can solve the customer's problem. Our first impulse when we hear an objection is to mutter something along the lines of: "Ohhelptheywillnot-buynowwhatamIgoingtodo?Iamgoingtodie!"

There is no need to die. This customer may well still buy. And you can surely help yourself if—whenever an objections rears its ugly head—you can remember this key maxim:

> *An objection is simply a request for more information.*

Why Prospective Customers Object

Prospective customers object for one simple reason: they do not believe that we have fully solved their problem. Perhaps we missed something in discovery—they tried to tell us but we did not hear them. The missed issue will show up as an objection somewhere in the sales process.

Another scenario: perhaps the sales process has helped the customer clarify his or her thinking about the purchase. The customer now knows things about what they want that they did not know when they walked in the door. The *customer* knows it, but *we* don't know it. Yet. The new information will pop up as an objection when we begin to make our case/present our solution. And it will show up because the solution we are proposing does not address this newly-identified component of the customer's problem.

Let's say we listened closely and did all our work thoroughly—does that make us bombproof when we make the case that we can solve the problem? Are we guaranteed there will be no objections? Sadly, no.

Objections can come for other reasons as well—perhaps the customer withheld a critical piece of information (financial constraints, key deadlines, who-knows-what) and then throws that information on the table immediately after you present your solution. You may have a bang-up solution, but your solution only addresses *part* of the problem. And now you have to deal with the new information that broadens your understanding of the problem.

A common temptation at this point is to panic. Don't give in—*an objection is not as big a deal as most salespeople believe.*

What Do I Do When I Get an Objection?

There has been a lot of nonsense written about objections—more perhaps than any other topic in selling, including closing. And the fallacy in most of this stuff is that it treats objections like a war of wills: *overcome* objections, *counter* objections, *take away* objections, *deny* objections. You and I are not going to go there—we never win if the customer loses, and each of the words above looks like a word designed to make the customer lose. All we need do is to remember:

> *An objection is simply a request for more information.*

Put another way, an objection is a simple question. And the core question underlying the objection is this: "But can you solve *this* part of my problem?" And "this part" of the problem could be any of myriad things: something they forgot to tell you, something you forgot to ask about, something they realized—but never mentioned—after you did your initial discovery with them.

So an objection is just a question? Fine. Then, what do we do with the question?

What does any rational person expect when she asks a question? She expects an answer. It's that simple. Answer the objection, then move back to the sales process, pick up with making your case/presenting the solution, and—barring other objections—ask for the order.

A Simple Process for Dealing with Objections

Fortunately for us, dealing with objections is not a mysterious art, accessible only to the initiated. Dealing with objections is a *skill*—a skill that each of us can build through study and practice. And building the skill for dealing with objections begins with recognizing the six steps that take us from hearing an objection through clarifying and addressing it, and then back into the sale we were making when the objection occurred. Here are the steps; take a quick look:

1. Pause and take a deep breath—don't panic!
2. Restate the objection.
3. Clarify the objection by probing.
4. Answer the objection.
5. Get confirmation that you have dealt fully with the objection.
6. Transition back to the sales process.

Let's look at these steps in turn—fleshing out our understanding of how each step fits into the process of dealing with objections, and exploring an example that will make the whole process concrete.

Pause and Take a Deep Breath

This is the most important step. Take a deep breath. This is not the end of the sale. Here is a chance for you to demonstrate —once again—how customer-focused you are. Remind yourself that *"An objection is simply a request for more information!"*

Remember that you don't win if the customer loses. Repeat: "The customer is not my enemy; we are both on the same side here." Then move to Step 2.

Restate the Objection

Repeat what you just heard the customer saying, softening the language if you think it will help the sale. For instance, a customer might say, "I've heard your quality really stinks!" You could restate and soften by saying, "So, you've got some concerns about quality?"

Clarify the Objection by Probing

Step 3 in the process is where you circle back to what you know about Discovery and gather the additional facts you need to address the customer's objection. This is a place to use your questioning skills as thoroughly as you ever have.

In the case of our prospective customer's concern about the quality of our product, here are some of the questions you might ask:

- What, specifically, concerns you about our quality?
- How do you think these concerns might play out in your use of the product?
- Do you have any data to support your concerns?
- Could I look at your data? We always like to see objective facts about our quality!
- What is/was the source of your information that indicated we have quality problems?

Answer the Objection

Now's the time to answer their question—directly and unambiguously. Provide supporting evidence (test results, lab reports, endorsements from satisfied customers) to buttress your answer. Make sure you deal with all parts of their objection. Don't ignore the part of the objection that you don't want to deal with, because it will not go away!

In the example where our customer has raised a quality issue, it might sound something like this:

> "I can appreciate your concern about quality—no one wants to change suppliers and then immediately have an issue with quality. I have some independent test results that demonstrate our product is better than—or equal to—all its leading competitors. I'll be happy to get you those reports...
>
> "All that, of course, is just laboratory stuff. You are probably much more interested in how the product performs in the real world, aren't you? (Customer nods.) I can give you three references of people who use our product in an application very similar to yours. Why don't you call them yourself, and see what they have to say? You can be sure they wouldn't use the product if it didn't work, because they've got to make a buck just like you do." (Do not offer current customers as references unless they have given you permission to do this!)

Get Confirmation from the Prospective Customer That You Have Dealt Fully with the Objection

Ask the customer—in plain English—if you have given them the information to answer their question. Remember: *"An objection is just a request for more information."* If you address the question completely, the objection will go away.

In our example here, the underlying question in the customer's mind is this: "If I buy this product, will I have problems with the quality?"

So the question you want to ask the prospective customer is "Has the information I've given you put your mind at ease about the quality of our products? And especially has it eased your concern about the use of the product in the application for which you intend it?"

Transition Back to the Sales Process

Once you answer the question that led to the objection, you have earned the right to reenter the sales process. Let's say the objection arose while you were in Making the Case in Step 5. You can make a seamless transition back to making the case with a statement something like this: "Interestingly, I'm glad you raised the quality issue and that we already have it on the table. One reason I think our product is better for your purposes than any of the other ones you are considering is our superior quality. Let's take a look at other reasons you might consider using our product..."

This six-step process will guide you in dealing successfully with any authentic objections you encounter. There are three key things to remember as you deal with objections:

1. Don't panic—panicked people cannot think clearly!
2. An objection is simply a request for more information.
3. When you get an objection—probe it (to fully understand it) before you address it.

Probing to Flush out Additional Objections

Customers almost always have objections; it's the nature of the business. Things come up, issues get missed in Discovery—there are a myriad of reasons a customer could legitimately object when you make the case that *your* solution is the *best* solution to this customer's problem. The good news is this: now that you know how to deal with them, handling objections can become one of the ways you distinguish yourself from your competition. In fact, it's sometimes a good idea to *invite* objections so that they get out on the table early.

As you move through the sales process, stop periodically to check for clarity and see if the customer has questions or concerns. This way, you can deal with the issues as you make your case, and co-opt them well before they pop-up as full-blown objections. And you might as well identify them now—objections never simply evaporate.

Questions I have used to flush out objections include:

- What concerns do you have so far?
- Is there anything about this approach that bothers you?
- When you think about this solution, what are your first thoughts?
- When you think about this solution, what are your first concerns?
- Why might this solution not work in the situation you face?
- How have you seen solutions like this fail in the past?

In each case, I was prompting the prospective customer to get him or her to help me identify things that will ultimately come up as objections. Then I deal with the objections here and now, rather than waiting for them to catch up to me later. I am practicing preventive medicine—dealing with a minor issue now before it festers into a major illness later on in the sales process.

As a friend of mine once said about this process: "Go ahead and cast a wide net. Pull in all the objections you can at once. Then filet them (solve them with support) one by one."

This is great counsel. Objections do not simply vanish. Invite them throughout the process and deal with them as they arise. It will build trust and credibility on the customer's part, and it will make your job easier at the close.

Phony Objections

"Phony Objections" are one of the most difficult challenges in the sales world. In a phony objection, the customer—for reasons that are not at all clear to us as salespeople—will not reveal what is really on his or her mind. You can usually recognize phony objections in one of two telltale ways:

1. A phony objection will be impossibly vague and amorphous, or
2. A phony objection will fly in the face of the data available and the case you have already made.

Phony objections could include any of the following:

- "I'm just not sure…"
- "Let me think about it…"
- "I need a couple of days…"
- "But what about…"
- "Let me ask so-and-so"

When we encounter a phony objection, our first step is to treat it exactly like a regular objection—assume at the outset that it is sincere and authentic. Use your six-step process that we just reviewed—at least up to point three where you probe the objection to see if you can clarify and fully understand it. Ask as many questions as possible to refine and clarify the objection so that you can address it in a rigorous way.

Your questions might include:

- "What, exactly, are you unsure about?"
- "What is it that you need to think about?"
- "What will you know in a couple of days that you do not know now?"
- "What information do you need that I have neglected to give you?"
- "Could you call so-and-so right now?"
- "What have I not made clear?"

Here's an important caution: as salespeople, we *always* take responsibility for whatever situation or miscommunication produced an objection. *Do not blame the customer for an objection*—even if you think the objection is phony. Just continue to pursue the germ of reality under the apparently phony objection. We don't win if the customer loses—and people who feel like they are being blamed think they are losing.

So your first step is to treat a possible phony objection just as you would any other objection. The customer will sometimes clarify the objection for you if you ask precise questions and probe thoroughly. If you *do* get enough clarity to grab the handle on the objection, that's great. Address the objection completely, check for agreement, and then move back into the sales process.

If the customer persists in his or her objection, there are two final approaches to try.

"I'm confused." In this approach, you look quizzically at the customer and say,

"I'm confused..." Then you recap your conversation to date: the problem the customer brought in, the solution you have identified, and the fact that they have agreed with you every step of the way. You recount the fact that you believe you have solved the problem, and you close your conversation with, "Given all this, I'm confused about why you are concerned. What's up?"

And then you wait. If they clarify, solve the problem they identify. If they don't, you can carefully move to Step 2 below.

"Something is missing here…" This approach to phony objections is a final step after "I'm confused…" If—after doing everything above—the customer persists in delaying the sale with excuses, you can just simply name what you see. It sounds something like this: "We've spent a fair amount of time together, and you said I had solved your problem with the solution I just presented. Now you seem reluctant to make the purchase. Something's missing from this picture; what is it?"

You may find that the customer—in the passion of the purchase—has committed to a product that he or she can't afford, or there may be some other factor blocking the final sale. Good! Now you know another constraint on the sale. Circle back to Discovery and identify other, unnamed constraints, and then begin the sale anew with the additional information you have. From this point on, proceed as if this was a regular sale.

Be cautious in how you deal with phony objections. Human beings like to *choose* when they buy—no one likes to be *pressured* into buying. The above tactics can be very helpful when used judiciously and with polish. Used inappropriately or aggressively, they can quickly escalate from objection to rejection and you will find yourself out on your butt.

Proceed carefully! And remember: you can't sell every customer. If you continue to be confronted with objections that fail the smell test, back off and let the customer go. If the objection is authentic, they'll return. If not, you've saved time to pursue other, more productive customers.

Dealing with Objections on Price

Customers often object on price—at least partly because price is the easiest part of the sale to quantify. Since price is so easy to measure, it is tempting to meet the competitor's price and get on with the sale. Resist this temptation and cut price only as a last resort. There are several important reasons not to cut price right out of the gate:

Price May Not be the Main Objection

It's merely the *first* objection. Get all the objections out on the table before you deal with any of them, or else you will have given away the store before you ever get to the main objection.

Cutting Price Kills Margins

Imagine an item that you can make for $1.00—including labor, materials, distribution, everything. You can sell this item for $2.00, so your mark-up is 100 percent and your profit margin is $1.00, or 50 percent. Simple math, and a not-uncommon mark-up percentage.

Now let's suppose that you are under pricing pressure from a competitor and you decide to cut your price to get the sale. You drop the price to $1.50—giving your customer a 25 percent price decrease. Simple enough, but *you just cut your dollar margin in half*—from $1.00 per unit to $.50 per unit. For you to break even on this price reduction, your customer will have to double his or her purchases!

Anytime you are tempted to cut price, do the math. Ask yourself: is this deal going to pay out? Then be careful before you move forward.

Cutting Price Messes up the Market

Know that your customers talk to each other. And they brag when they get a good price on anything.

Cutting prices for one customer will quickly lead to pricing erosion for other, similar customers. And it will lead to a host of questions if a major customer finds that another, smaller customer is getting a better price.

Pricing integrity is hard to maintain. But it's even harder to deal with all the issues that arise when price cutting is undisciplined and gets out of hand. Cut your price with fear and trembling—*and* only as a last resort.

Bringing in a Colleague

Most of the time, the processes we have laid out here will allow you to answer a prospective customer's questions and remove the objections that are caused by those questions. The operative phrase here is "most of the time" because occasionally you will meet an objection that baffles even you. It may be one you have never heard or one that seems perfectly reasonable to you and for which you have no response. Either way, the response is the same: bring in a colleague.

I once heard someone say—about selling and about objections:

> *"If you get in trouble, probe. If you stay in trouble, call in a colleague."*

We've already talked about probing—the careful asking of questions to fully understand an objection so we can address it professionally. Now let's take a quick run at calling in a colleague. This is a process that is sometimes called the "turnover" since we are turning the prospective customer over to someone else because of the impasse we have reached with the customer.

A turnover can be a good idea for a number of reasons. First, you have already acknowledged that you can't solve the problem. Now you can call in an expert who can solve the problem, and you can position yourself as the fellow traveler/companion who found the expert who could answer the prospective customer's question.

Another advantage of doing a turnover is that it allows you to back away a little bit from the sales interaction. You have been so close to this customer and this sale that a little perspective is often helpful. As your colleague works with the customer, you can listen carefully and observe closely—it almost becomes a clinic in selling. Often you will see or hear something you missed—the very something that may be holding up the sale. Then you can move in and help the customer answer his or her question and move towards consummating the sale.

A final advantage of calling in a colleague when a sale gets stuck is that it gives you another perspective on the customer. Your colleague doubtless knows things you don't know, and will see and hear things a little differently from you. The two of you—working in tandem—have a better chance of addressing the customer's objection, answering the customer's questions, and solving the customer's problem than you do working on your own. And after all, those three things are the raison d'être for the entire sales interaction.

Remember: *honest* objections are always about unanswered questions. Identify and answer the question (or have a colleague answer it on your behalf), and you have a good shot at making the sale. Call in a colleague. Turnover when you reach an impasse. Solve the problem and make the sale!

Watch for "Buying Signs"

All the time that you are dealing with objections, you are also watching for *buying signs*. A buying sign is just that—a sign from the customer that he or she feels like you have made the case for your product, and that your product will solve the problem that brought them in the door in the first place.

Buying signs take many forms, but all buying signs indicate that the customer is beginning to envision himself or herself as the owner of the product. As an example, suppose you have been showing furniture to a young couple with several small children. They seemed excited about the items you had shown them until someone raised the issue of stain resistance for the fabric. With small children, this is a key issue, though it had not come up in the discovery portion of the sale.

You walked them to the swatch book and showed them the many fabric choices you had available—dozens of which had been treated with the industry's leading stain repellant treatment. This is where you met their objection and answered their previously unanswered question. And they immediately began to demonstrate buying behavior when they started a spirited discussion about which fabric would look best in their recently repainted family room.

Buying signs can take many forms, but they often deal with price, financing, availability for delivery, options (as in the fabric choices), and other things related to getting the product as *I want it, when I want it, where I want it, and the price I wanted.* Some typical buying signs might include statements or questions like these:

- Can I get one exactly like this but in a different color/fabric?
- When can you make delivery? Do you charge for delivery?
- What APR are you charging these days?
- Can you deliver it today?
- How much discount do you give for cash?
- How much "wiggle room" do you have in that price?
- How much will you give me as a trade allowance?
- I really like this one, but I have a better price from another vendor...

You may also occasionally hear buying signs that indicate a product is "perfect." These are so easy to recognize that I only give a few examples here for completeness:

- "Honey, wouldn't this be perfect in our dining room?"
- "This is exactly what I was looking for!"

Whenever you hear buying signs, it's time to jump to chapter 10 and Ask for the Order! You may get an objection when you do this, but *now* you know what to do when the prospective customer objects!

Using the Trial Close to Transition Back to the Sales Process

A "trial close" is just that—it's a time when you try to close with this customer. Many people who teach selling infuse this process with lots of mystery and hocus-pocus, but it's actually quite simple.

> *In a trial close, you get agreement that something has been solved.*
> *(In fact, the agreement is the close. You are closing on the proposition that "I have solved this part of your problem.")*

The final close for any sale exists at the end of the sales process—it's the point where the customer agrees to buy and the salesperson "closes" the sale. In the language of our catchphrase above, "In the final close, you get agreement that everything has been solved."

Truth be told, however, salespeople are closing from the minute they first encounter the customer. In fact, one of the most important closes in the whole sales process occurs in the meet and greet, when the salesperson closes the customer on the notion that the salesperson is a "credible colleague." And—if the salesperson can't close on the issue of credibility—the rest of the process is a waste of time. The only way a customer will buy from a salesperson with no credibility is if the salesperson has a demonstrably better product at a significantly lower price. And it's hard to make a living selling markedly better goods for far less money.

So we are closing from the moment we meet the customer—closing that we can serve them better than anyone else, closing that we have heard them and fully understand their issues, closing that we can meet their needs and solve their problems. So what, exactly, is a "trial close"?

A trial close is an attempt to see if we have solved the problem or met the objection a customer has raised, and to see if he or she is ready to move back to the overall sales process. Usually a trial close can be done very simply—with just a phrase or two. Here are some sample trial closes that have worked for me:

- Well, what do you think?
- So, how does that sound?
- Does what we have talked about deal with your concerns?
- With this as background, would you say I have dealt with your issue?

It is important to be purposeful about using trial closes as you deal with objections. You want to close on the objection and be able to move smoothly back into the sale itself. But trial closing is not especially complex. It's a simple matter of asking—either directly or obliquely—"Have I solved this part of your problem?" Once you have solved at least part of their problem, head back to the sales process, move logically through the balance of the sales process, and ask for the order.

Reasons to Take Heart

The Objections step is probably the most fear-inducing part of the entire sales process. I am asking you to let go of that fear, and see objections as a logical step on the path from making the case to getting the order. Think about it this way: an objection means the customer is listening to you and taking what you say seriously. It means they care enough about the deal to point out places that the deal might jump the track. It means they have given you a second chance to deal with an issue that they did not feel got addressed in the initial interaction.

Objections are a good—not a bad—thing. That doesn't mean they are always easy. But neither is labor in childbirth, and you wouldn't be here if your mom hadn't been willing to go through *that*!

Getting Down to Cases: A Quick Content Review on Objections

1. Where can objections occur in the sales process? ______
______

2. What often provides the impetus for an objection to occur? ______

3. Fill in the blanks: *"An objection is simply a ______ for more ______."*

4. What are the six steps in dealing with an objection? List them below:
   1.
   2.
   3.
   4.
   5.
   6.

5. Why do objections occur? ______

6. How can you separate a phony objection from an authentic objection? ______

7. Fill in the blanks: "If you get in trouble ______, if you stay in trouble ______ ______."

Making It Real: Applying What You Learned about Objections to the Sales You Have to Make

Remember my covenant with you: I'm going to give you every opportunity to learn how to sell the product that feeds your family. I can't do the work for you, but I can provide you with an opportunity to do your own work and internalize the concepts that will make you a better salesperson.

Take a few minutes and reflect on the product or service you sell, then answer these questions about dealing with objections. Life is not a closed book exam; feel free to review the material in the chapter as you deal with these questions. But please write your answers out in the spaces provided—it helps load the material to the hard drive of your brain.

1. How do you most commonly respond when you hear an objection? Does your common response work for you? Why did you answer as you did?

2. What are the most common objections you hear in the selling you do? List three to five of them in the space below.

3. What causes objections to arise in the selling you do? What have you found that works to help prevent or deal with objections as they arise?

4. What probing questions work best in your experience? List three of them below.

5. What has been your experience dealing with phony objections? What works best for you in dealing with this special challenge?

6. What are the special cautions we noted regards dealing with phony objections? Refer to the chapter and write them below. (They can also be found in the "Key Reminders" section on the next page.)

7. Before reading this chapter, were you familiar with the notion of a "Turnover"? Have you ever used a Turnover to make a sale? How might it be helpful?

8. What is a trial close, and how can they be helpful in dealing with objections and transitioning back to the sales process?

Key Reminders

- Objections can occur at any point in the sales process.
- Making the case often causes objections to surface.
- An objection is almost always a request for more information.
- Prospective customers object for one simple reason: they do not believe we have fully solved their problem.
- Put another way, an objection is a simple question. And the core question underlying the objection is this: "But can you solve this part of my problem?"
- Don't panic when you hear an objection! Just circle back to Discovery and begin gathering more data.
- If you get in trouble, probe. If you stay in trouble, call in a colleague.
- Watch for buying signs, then ask for the order.

10

It's Okay to Ask for the Order

Okay, here's the one thing no one ever told you about selling—the thing you would not have dared to imagine on your own.

> *If you work the sales process faithfully, closing is the easiest step!*

There—I've said it.

Closing is *not* black magic. You do not have to sacrifice a young calf on the full moon to the god of sales success. You do not have to trick 'em into buying. You do not even have to memorize 101 all-purpose closes. All you have to do is listen closely, follow the steps in the sales process, and solve the customer's problem. *If you do these things faithfully, the sale will probably close itself.*

Remember that selling is a series of commitments. If you get a commitment at each point in the sales process, you will have earned the right to close. And your customer will likely buy from you, because buying from you solves his or her problem better than any of the other options that are available.

How Does Closing Fit into the Overall Sales Process?

Let's walk back through the sales model one more time. We'll see where we are, what has happened before we reach the closing step, and how we can make sure that we reap the results of all the hard work we have done by the time we get to closing. Take a look at Figure 10-1 and see what has happened as we have moved through the steps of the sales process.

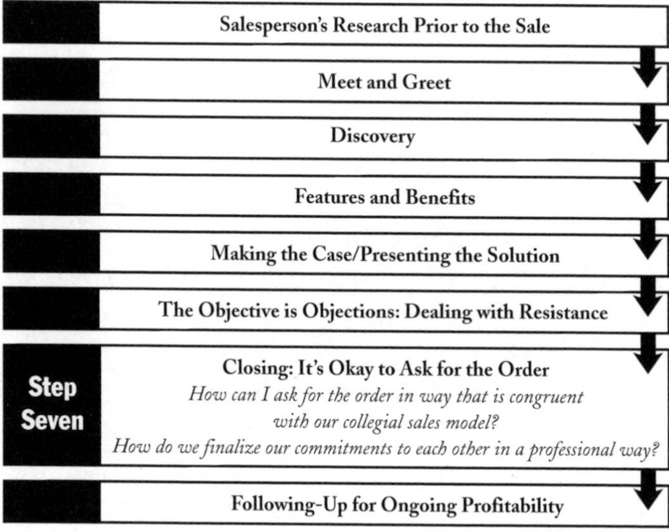

Salesperson's Research Prior to the Sale
Meet and Greet
Discovery
Features and Benefits
Making the Case/Presenting the Solution
The Objective is Objections: Dealing with Resistance
Step Seven
Closing: It's Okay to Ask for the Order
How can I ask for the order in way that is congruent with our collegial sales model?
How do we finalize our commitments to each other in a professional way?
Following-Up for Ongoing Profitability

Figure 10-1

Closing is near the very end of the entire process—we have done most of our hard work by the time we arrive here. We have learned all about our products and about our competitors in Step 1, and we have made a credible first impression in Step 2. We have used Steps 3 and 4 to fully understand the buyer's problem, and to present the key features about our product that help to solve the prospective customer's problem. We have made the case that our product will solve the prospect's problem, and we have dealt with resistance as it popped up. And now we have to close, otherwise all that hard work goes to waste.

Most times we are afraid, and we sweat. Our mouth grows dry, and the words stick in it. But all this anxiety is pointless because—truth be told—if we have done our jobs up to this point, the entire closing will go smoothly.

If we have earned the right to close, then closing is just one more commitment in a logical series of commitments.

Closing as a Series of Commitments

The close of a sale is the last step in a long line of steps that have helped to build a relationship between you and the prospective customer. In this way, the close is similar to the example from the world of dating that we cited much earlier in our work together.

Few among us would drop to one knee and propose to someone in the second hour of a first date. The proposal is the "close" of a dating relationship—it speaks to knowing one another and being willing to do business (the business of building a home and a family) with one another over the course of a lifetime. It is a big commitment. And few of us would ask for this commitment (or make it, for that matter) after the first hour of the first date. And so it is, too, with buying.

Prospective customers are rarely willing to make the commitment to buy early in the selling process. They have to tell you their problem, and you have to hear their circumstances in a way that makes you a credible partner in their problem solving. You have to hear their concerns, and then build trust with them that you are—of all the available suppliers—best able to solve their concerns. Only then, after this series of step-by-step commitments has been made, do people find themselves ready to make the big commitment: to accept the proposal, to write the check, to sign the lease, to risk changing from a familiar supplier to one with whom they have no experience.

Closing (and selling) is a series of commitments. Each commitment moves the prospective buyer and the salesperson closer together as a team, and closer to their joint objective of solving the customer's problem so the salesperson can make a sale. Commitments that are kept strengthen the relationship; commitments that are broken threaten to rupture the relationship and put everyone's hard work in the trash bin.

The single best way to move a sale along towards a successful close is to *keep your commitments*: underpromise and overdeliver on every commitment you make to your prospective customer. Do what you say you will do, when you said you would do it. In this way you heighten your credibility as a problem-solving partner working *with* the customer to solve the problem that took him or her into the market in the first place.

Figure 10-2 on the next page provides you with insight into the types of commitments that we make (and seek) at each stage of the sales process. Be sure you monitor the commitments you "owe" your buyer at each stage of the process, and don't forget to solicit commitments from the customer as well. Among the commitments you could elicit from a buyer: a commitment to buy from you when you *do* solve the problem, a commitment to give you one last shot at beating a competitor's offer, and any other commitments that seem to bring the relationship into some kind of equity.

Remember: selling is a two-way relationship. It is appropriate to *seek* as well as *offer* commitments—as an indication of reciprocity and goodwill between you and your customer. If you are committed to *serving* the customer while they are only committed to *screwing* you then things are surely going to go south eventually!

Commitments Made in the Sales Process

Step 1—Research Prior to the Sale

Salesperson Commitment(s)

- To fully understand his or her own product
- To fully understand all competitive products
- To understand all applications and uses of each of the products, and of all products that could be used instead of the salesperson's product

Customer Commitment(s)

- None—no customer in sight. All of the salesperson's work in Step 1 is presale research.

Step 2—Meet and Greet

Salesperson Commitment(s)

- To meet the customer and listen to his or her story
- To be trustworthy

Customer Commitment(s)

- To be trustworthy
- To value the salesperson's time and not jerk him or her around

Figure 10-2

Step 3—Discovery

Salesperson Commitment(s)

- To question carefully and fully understand the problem
- To value the customer's understanding of the problem
- To address root causes, not symptoms
- To help the customer find the best solution to the problem

Customer Commitment(s)

- To describe the problem as fully as possible
- To disclose all relevant information that could impact the sale

Step 4—Features and Benefits

Salesperson Commitment(s)

- To speak only in terms that matter to the customer
- To "bridge" each feature to a benefit that the customer cares about
- To focus on features and benefits that solve the customer's problem

Customer Commitment(s)

- To identify the things that matter and the things that don't matter
- To assign some relative importance to each attribute of the problem, so the salesperson can know what matters most.

Step 5—Making the Case/Presenting the Solution

Salesperson Commitment(s)

- To present an option that solves the customer's problem(s)
- To check-in with the customer and get a response while presenting the proposed solution

Customer Commitment(s)

- To listen to the salesperson's proposed solution
- To raise issues of concern in a rational way

Step 6—Objections: Dealing with Resistance

Salesperson Commitment(s)

- To listen to/value each objection—not to dismiss any objection out-of-hand
- To probe and fully understand each objection
- To respond professionally and in problem-solving mode to each objection
- To check back to see if each objection has been addressed fully

Customer Commitment(s)

- To raise objections as they occur, and not to sit on or stockpile them
- To raise the real objection and not jerk the salesperson around with phony objections/resistance to the sale.

Step 7—Closing

Salesperson Commitment(s)

- To tell the truth
- To make sure the problem is solved before trying to close
- Not to use manipulative closes in reaching for the order

Customer Commitment(s)

- To buy if the salesperson solves the problem in a way that works best for the customer
- To tell the truth about reasons for not buying if the sale doesn't close

Step 8—Follow-Up

Salesperson Commitment(s)

- To keep all commitments made in closing the sale
- To maintain appropriate contact with the customer after the sale is made
- Not to use the customer as a reference without permission

Customer Commitment(s)

- To keep all commitments made in the sale
- To surface after-sale problems with the salesperson before escalating them up the management chain

So How, Exactly, Do We Close the Sale and Ask for the Order?

There are as many ways to close a sale and ask for the order as there are to do anything else in life. But I'd suggest you close in the easiest way possible: In English, if that's your native tongue, and with a simple question.

Think about the circumstances that surround your having finally reached the point of closing the sale. You have been working with your prospective customer for some time now. You have listened carefully to the problem(s) that brought him or her into the market, and you have done your best to solve that problem. You have asked for feedback, and likely handled at least one objection from the customer.

You know that the customer is not your enemy, and you don't win if they lose. You are a team, and the two of you have been chipping away at the problem almost since the meet and greet. You seem to have reached consensus that the problem has been identified and solved. The next step is to close the sale. What in the world do you say? The words clutch in your throat as you struggle to get them out.

Do not panic. It's far simpler than you think. All you need to say at this point is: "So, what do you think?"

And that's all there is to closing.

If the customer is ready to buy, he or she will say, "It sounds good to me." Then you can write up the sale and move on to keep the commitments you have made in the sales process. If the customer is not ready to buy, the close will flush out an objection and you can circle back to deal with this new-found objection by probing and using the pointers we covered in chapter 9. Either way, the sale is moving forward.

It's Okay to Ask for the Order—Really

I am unclear why or how we have gotten our underpants into such a wad about this notion of closing. Just for kicks, let's review. You encountered a potential buyer with a problem. You offered to help the buyer solve his problem and—if you followed the steps fully—spent a fair amount of time listening to his problem, understanding his problem, and selecting/presenting a solution to his problem. And now you are saying—in effect—"If you do this (if you buy this product or service from me) your problem will be solved."

Who in the world is ever mad when you help them solve their problems?

Closing—at least the kind of closing we are learning in this sales process—is not some magical, mysterious process fraught with fear and danger. Closing is the logical next step in a process of solving the customer's problem—a process that began long before you met the customer.

You've solved the problem. You've earned the right to close. It's okay to ask for the order—*really!*

What Happens If They Say "No"?

Sometimes the customer will say no when you try to close, but that's no cause for panic. You already know what to do here—just follow the steps. *"No" is an objection.* It's not a very useful one, by the way, because it is not specific enough to be helpful, but it is an objection nonetheless. What do we do when we get an objection? *We probe it*—you've already learned that! So...

> *If you get in trouble or hear "no" when you try to close, go back to Discovery and probe.*

What Happens after the Customer Says "Yes"?

Chapter 11 will take a look at all that happens in the follow-up—the final step in the selling process. For now, though, let's take a look at what happens in the few minutes immediately after the customer says, "Sounds good to me."

First, you are overcome—if not with euphoria, at least with relief. You have been waiting for this moment and now it's here. Even though you know that you are in business to solve customer problems, *you are also fundamentally evaluated on the sales you make.* If you solve customer problems without making any sales, eventually you have problems of your own.

So you are relieved—but what does that have to do with the customer?

He or she is likely relieved, too—and perhaps more than a little anxious ("Did I make the right decision?") Our tasks immediately after the sale include:

1. Celebrating with the customer in his or her relief, and
2. Moving immediately to allay all anxiety (sales theorists call it "cognitive dissonance") that accompanies making a final selection from many competing options.

How do we celebrate? Easy enough—congratulate the customer on his or her choice, and assure her or him that you think they will "be very pleased with their choice." If you are selling face-to-face this is often the place for a celebratory meal, or at least a cup of coffee to consummate the deal. If you are not face-to-face, this is nevertheless the place to pause, celebrate the customer's purchase, and congratulate him or her on their good judgment in choosing to do business with you.

Then move immediately to allay any anxiety that could come up for the customer. It's not unusual for folks to have second thoughts when they have made a difficult choice from multiple, high-ticket, competing options. Think about your own experience in buying cars, homes, or even clothing. Don't you ever find yourself thinking: "Wonder if I would have been happier if I had chosen the other one?" Your customers are no different from you in this regard!

Consequently, we move immediately to *dispel anxiety* in a simple but effective way, *using the three R's of anxiety reduction:*

1. *Recap* all your agreements,
2. *Review* the benefits to the customer of decisions made (and how it solves the problem that brought them into the market in the first place), then
3. *Reduce* all commitments to writing.

Using the three Rs will reinforce your customer's choice. Their post-sale anxiety bubble will deflate, and they will leave the closing assured that buying from you was the best possible choice they could have made! (In addition—*if* you keep all the commitments you have made—these customers will become an excellent source of referrals.)

Selling Secret 202

You can close at any point in the sales process. But you have to read the cues carefully. I almost didn't tell you this part. (Sometimes it is easier not to tell everything you know. Abraham Lincoln is reputed to have once spoken to this topic by saying, "You ought to always tell the truth. But you don't have to always be telling it!")

However, to withhold this gem about selling would be to break my covenant with you. You wanted to learn how to sell. You bought the book. I promised to teach you. So here goes.

You can close at any point in the sales process—even at the meet and greet stage. You can't skip the commitments that have to be made prior to the sale, but—once they are made—you can close whenever your customer is ready.

This situation may be hard to envision; let me give you an example. Suppose you work for an office machine company. You have been calling on a high-value prospect for years, but to no good effect. This prospective customer was happy, they knew they had a good deal, and they had no reason to change suppliers. (That would put them in Quadrant 2 from the Problem-Awareness Grid in chapter 8: doesn't have a problem and knows s/he doesn't have a problem.) You continued to build a relationship with the customer, and you waited patiently for their current supplier to stumble.

One fine spring day, you get a call from the obviously irate purchasing manager at your prospective customer. He or she quickly rattles off the specifics of a contract while you take frantic notes. Then you hear the question you've waited for all this time: "Can you match this?" This is the time to take a deep breath, and to make sure you fully understand the contract and all its particulars. Because if you do understand it, you can close this sale with your next comment.

You look closely at the sheet in front of you and then you reply, "I not only can match it, I believe I can beat it by a bit. What do you think? When should we sign the contract?"

By all appearances you have just sold this customer in the meet and greet—and by phone, no less. Of course you and I know that you have been building a relationship (and keeping commitments) with this customer for months—perhaps even years. But you *did* make the final close in two minutes—by phone. Because you had built rapport, the customer trusted you. And the customer knew you were willing to solve his or her problem.

Occasionally you can make a sale in the meet and greet

even when you have never seen the customer before your first encounter. I have a good friend who is an excellent salesperson (salespeople are an especially tough sell—you know that yourself) and who likes to drive expensive cars. He was looking for a Mercedes some years back and—because he is who he is—he had *really* done his homework.

By the time he was finished, he knew the model number, engine size, paint color, and a hundred other details about the car he wanted. He knew what kind of sound system he wanted, the type of transmission, and every other possible detail about his dream car. Then he typed up a bid sheet, faxed it to every Mercedes dealer in a three-hundred mile radius, and waited for phone calls. He bought the car from someone he had never met—and he bought it in a five-minute phone call. The sale went straight from the meet and greet to the close. Or did it?

Reflect for a minute: did this sale really happen in the meet and greet? My friend did most of the heavy lifting for the salesperson: he defined the problem, he wrote the specs, he told prospective suppliers what they had to do ("Give me this car at the lowest net price, delivered.") to get the sale. There was no need for discovery, the customer already knew the features and benefits, and the case was made.

My friend's only "problem" (remember: customers buy to solve a problem) was that he did not know who had the lowest price. His bid process solved that problem, and the person with the lowest price won the sale in a five-minute conversation. My friend turned the sale of a high-line European automobile into an auction, and he took the lowest bidder. This is the very same reason purchasing agents ask for bids all the time.

Benediction: It's Not as Hard as They Said It Was

Many things are harder than they look (windsurfing comes to mind, plus golf, snowboarding, and a host of others). We most often see them done on television, by people who know all the tricks, and have honed their skills through years of hard practice. So—when we try it—the sport is far harder than we ever imagined.

Some people think the same thing is true about closing a sale—that it's deathly difficult.

Well, it's not.

Follow the steps and solve the customer's problem. Probe objections so you can get at the core kernel that drives the objection. Then *ask for the order*. Simply and in English. You'll be surprised how many sales you get.

Getting Down to Cases: A Quick Content Review

Now it's time to see if you got what you came for—if you can't close, then you can't sell and I've wasted your time and money with this book. So let's take a run at it. Answer the questions below and see what you've learned and how you will apply it.

1. What commitments—in your selling—do you make to the customer as you move through the sales process? List at least four. ____________________
   ____
   ____

2. Salespeople often panic when they have to ask for the order. But we have said that there is really no need to panic. Fill in the blanks in the sentences below to remind yourself why there is no need to panic.

"Selling and closing are just a series of ____________. If I ____________ the right to close, there will be no problem. In fact, if I work the ____________ faithfully, I will find that closing is the ____________ step of the entire process."

3. Asking for the order seems like such a big step, but it really is the next logical step after listening to the prospective customer, understanding the customer's

problem, talking purposefully about features and benefits, and dealing with objections. As we discussed, one way to ask for the customer's order is to say, "So, what do you think?"

What other closing phrases have you used successfully (or seen used successfully by other salespeople?) List at least three.

•

•

•

•

•

4. When is the best time to close a sale? ____________

____

____

5. What should you do if you get a "no" when you try to close the sale? ____________________________

____

____

6. What is the natural first response when the customer says "yes" to your close? ____________________

____

____

7. What is cognitive dissonance? Why does it occur? List below the "three Rs" that we use to help prevent —or diminish—cognitive dissonance.

R ______________________________________

R ______________________________________

R ______________________________________

8. What have you learned in this chapter that will help you do a better job asking for the order? List at least four things below. You are welcome to flip back through the chapter for reference. ______________

____

____

Key Reminders

- If you work the process faithfully, closing is the easiest step in the sales process.
- Closing is a series of commitments.
- If you get a commitment at each point in the sales process, you will have earned the right to close.
- When you've solved the problem. You've earned the right to close.
- Closing creates anxiety for the salesperson; buying creates anxiety for the customer.
- If you get in trouble in the close, go back to Discovery and see what you missed.
- Once you have closed the sale, do two things quickly:
    1. Celebrate with—and encourage—your buyer, and
    2. Move to allay the buyer's anxiety by locking down your commitments.
- The "three Rs" (Recap all your agreements, Review the benefits to the customer of decisions made, Reduce all commitments to writing) can go a long way towards reducing the customer's anxiety about the purchase.

Sales Step Eight

11

Following-Up for Ongoing Profitability

Follow-up is one of the hardest parts of the entire selling process. This is not because follow-up is so difficult per se, but because it requires a somewhat different skill set than selling itself.

Much of selling builds on the exact skill set—stalking, flushing, encountering—that our forebears developed thousands of years ago to hunt. Now I *know* I have said, "We don't win if the customer loses"—we are not here to *kill* customers. Even so, the analogy holds; the skill sets *do* overlap.

To be successful in selling, we have to find and pursue our customers, we have to study their behavior and anticipate their moves. And both selling and hunting—when successful—offer an adrenaline rush unparalleled in the world of *legal* pharmaceuticals.

And then there's follow-up. Hunting is exciting and stressful, and it culminates in one climactic moment when all our hard work yields a spectacular pay-off. Selling is very similar—it's a binary, yes/no, on/off, black/white enterprise

—you either get the sale or you don't. Follow-up, on the other hand, is like cleaning the animal you have just stalked and taken—it's messy, it goes on forever, and there is no moment of climax when you can thrust your fist in the air and holler *yes*!

Follow-up can be made into a routine; it seems predictable and boring to adrenaline junkies (that's us salespeople—or many of us anyway) who thrive on making the sale. Follow-up is everything that the initial sale wasn't, and that's why many salespeople lose interest, lose focus, and—eventually—lose the customer. And just as in hunting (where you don't get to eat if you don't clean the game you have taken) in selling you can't continue to feed your family from a sale unless you follow-up and do what needs doing after the sale.

It's too bad that all this is so hard for salespeople to understand. Because—for all their differences from the initial sale—follow-up sales have a critical similarity to that first, initial, climactic sale: *follow-up is all about solving customer problems*. And the salesperson who solves the prospective customer's problems—and *keeps them solved*—gets to keep the business.

Beyond the task of satisfying the customer, follow-up sales can also be the most profitable sales for you and for your organization. There is a host of estimates on the cost to acquire a new customer, and these estimates vary widely in range. But the most conservative estimates peg the cost of a conquest sale (the taking of a customer from a competitive supplier) at five-to-eight times the cost of a repeat sale (subsequent sales to a customer who is already on our customer roster.) It's the sale after the sale that makes you the most money.

Even in businesses where the sale appears to be episodic (automobiles, real estate, etc.) the second sale is far easier than the first one *if the follow-up has been done professionally and as promised.* The satisfied customer has "bought" the salesperson and his business proposition. The customer truly believes the salesperson is in the business of solving customer problems. On subsequent encounters the salesperson's only challenge is to fully understand the customer's *current* problem and to select a product (a vehicle, a property) that solves the customer's problem *this time.* And the satisfied customer can also be an excellent source of referrals to other prospective customers. But all this depends on follow-up...

How Does Follow-Up Fit into Our Sales Process?

Follow-up is the last step in our eight-step selling process, as you will see in Figure 11-1. It is the caboose on the train, coming at the end of the long trip from presale research through making the case to dealing with objections and closing. Interestingly—like many "last steps"—follow-up tends to get short shrift in most treatments of selling.

This is a shame; there are lots of customers to be satisfied (and lots of money to be made!) in doing follow-up well. It's also a shame that most salespeople see follow-up only as a *last* step—when follow-up also represents the beginning step for the next sale to this same customer or company. Take a quick look below to reorient yourself to the sales process. Find Step 8 and you've located follow-up. Pay special attention to the full name of this step: "Following-Up for Ongoing Profitability." We follow-up because it's the right thing to do: for the customer *and* for us. Don't forget—there's money to be made if we do this step well!

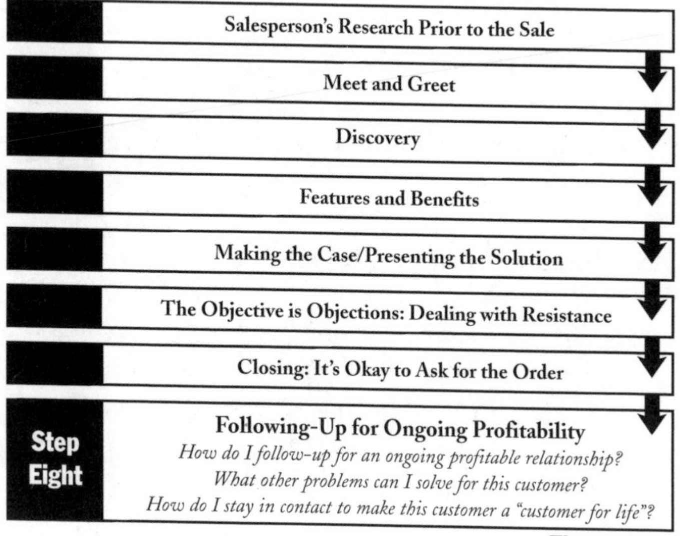

Salesperson's Research Prior to the Sale
Meet and Greet
Discovery
Features and Benefits
Making the Case/Presenting the Solution
The Objective is Objections: Dealing with Resistance
Closing: It's Okay to Ask for the Order
Step Eight
Following-Up for Ongoing Profitability
How do I follow-up for an ongoing profitable relationship?
What other problems can I solve for this customer?
How do I stay in contact to make this customer a "customer for life"?

Figure 11-1

Reframing Follow-Up as the First Step in the Next Sale

Because human beings live in linear time (one event follows another in sequence) we often segment and compartmentalize processes to make sense of them. That's what we have done here with selling, and it's a useful first step in wrapping our mind around the entire sales process. But the truth of sales is that *selling is more circular than linear* (witness how we circled back to discovery and probed every time we got an objection). Similarly, we saw that it is sometimes possible (though it is uncommon) to circle directly to closing from the meet and greet.

Figure 11-2 on the next page recasts our sales process as a circle, with excellent follow-up leading directly to discovery (in the case of repeat sales to a current customer) or to meet and greet (in the case of first sales to a referral sent to us from a satisfied customer). Take a quick look to lock this process in your mind. Good follow-up can be the key to filling your prospect pipeline with people who are predisposed to buy from you. How can that be a bad thing?

The Circular Sales Process: A More Accurate Representation

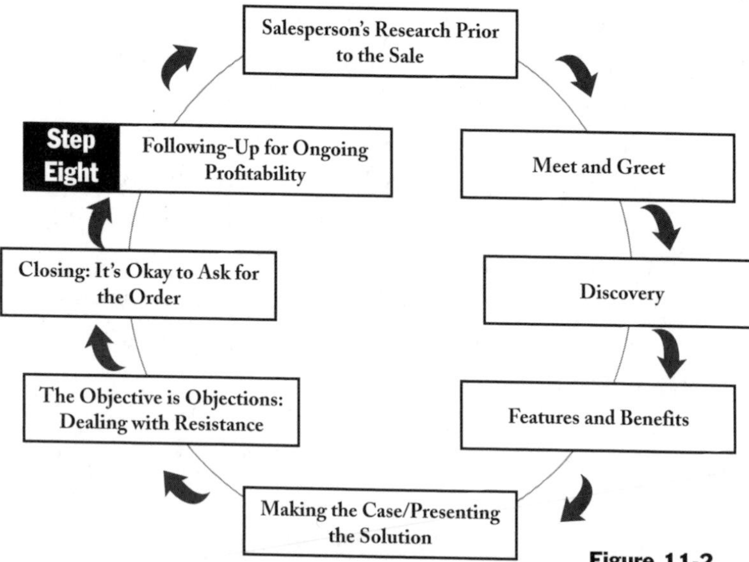

Figure 11-2

Keep Your Commitments—The Cardinal Rule of Selling

Keep your commitments. Do what you say you will do. Under-promise and over-deliver. All these are admonitions designed to manage around the all-too-human tendency to *let things slide* once the sale is made. It's not so much that salespeople (folks like you and me) are lying, dissembling, disingenuous twits—at least not in *my* case! It's just that the thrill of the hunt is more exciting than the drudgery of field dressing and cleaning the kill. But you can't eat the game if you don't do both, and you can't succeed in selling if you don't follow-up and keep your commitments. So do it, already.

Write it down! That's the best advice I can give to anyone in selling, or most of life for that matter. We make a grave mistake when we assume we know what others are going to do, or when we allow them to assume they know what we are going to do. Written agreements solve this problem, because they spell out, in clear terms, who is going to do what, for whom, by when, using what resources.

You would never contract with a builder to construct a new home for you and your family without some kind of contract. The contract spells out the final price, who has liability for what, when progress payments will be made, and a variety of other items. The contract—along with detailed plans/blueprints—gives both you and the builder a track to run on as you work together. These two documents help to frame your joint expectations of who will do what, for whom, by when, using what resources—and at what level of compensation.

In the same way that the contractor is building you a house, you and the new customer are building a relationship built on mutual understanding and exchange of value. (The customer sends money; you send goods and services in return for that money.)

I am not arguing here for a full-blown contract that takes days to draft and makes your attorneys rich. What I am saying is this: you have to sign a repair order at the car dealership when you have the slightest work—even an oil change—done on your car. If you have a written agreement for an oil change and a tire rotation, shouldn't you at least have some written record of this sale that has taken so much effort to close? Shouldn't you and the customer reduce to writing who is going to do what, for whom, by when, using what resources, and at what price, so there is a reduced likelihood that you will disappoint each other?

Put your agreement in writing. It will save a lot of weeping and wailing and gnashing of teeth on both sides of the transaction.

Selling the New Customer to Internal Contacts

Remember our quote from chapter 5:

> *"Using the jawbone of an ass, Samson was able to slay a thousand men.*
> *In like manner, we kill a thousand sales every day!"*

The risk of killing a sale with the jawbone of an ass seems to be especially pernicious when we turn over our hard-earned customers to internal folks in our organization —people who have not sweated blood to make the sale and to earn the customer's business. I am not making our internal staff evil, bad, or malicious. I am simply saying that they sometimes do not value our customers as much as we value our customers. And the cost of this behavior can be *very* high.

There is a solution to this situation, however, and it's quite simple: sell your new customer to any internal personnel who will serve the customer. Let the internal people know the value of the customer—how much the customer is buying initially, and their potential purchases over the life of the relationship. Help the customer service team *value* the customer—both for the business they do in the here and now, and for the business they could do in the days to come.

In many ways—and this is why as salespeople we sometimes feel so smushed—we are the ones who absorb all the blows from both sides of the sales interaction. We have to sell our product and our company to the prospective buyer, *and* we have to sell our new customers to the internal colleagues who will service the account once we have acquired it.

My favorite image for this predicament is the pad of cartilage in your knee—the one that cushions the knee joint between the thighbone and the bones of the lower leg. This pad is under tremendous strain—bearing weight from the femur above, and getting pressure from the tibia and fibula below. This is the very pad that keeps the bones of the knee from grinding on each other, and helps the joint work smoothly and without friction.

Your job as a salesperson is to ensure that your customer's interactions with your company are smooth and without friction. Sell the new customer to the your internal customer-care team so these folks don't "slay your customers with the jawbone of an ass!"

The Relationship Web

Just as you want to "sell" any new customers to the key internal service-people in your organization, you also want to sell yourself to multiple points-of-contact inside all your major accounts. Perhaps this example will amplify what I am talking about:

You phone a major customer—it's only been a week since you last talked with them—and ask for your key (and *only*) contact. The receptionist replies, "I'm sorry, he/she is no longer with our company. Is there someone else who can help you?" Your mind reels—what *am* I going to do now? Is there anything scarier in the business world than this scenario?

This is not a rhetorical question, and the answer is *No!* There is nothing scarier to a salesperson than hearing a key contact has left a valued and important customer. Your mind boggles with an assault of questions:

- Who will replace my key contact and strongest advocate?
- Will they bring their own favorite suppliers with them?
- How much at-risk is the sales number I had forecasted for this account?
- How do I protect my position in this account?
- Whom do I call now?
- Where did my contact go—and why?
- Can I sell my product to my contact at her/his new company?

While the last two questions above hint at some additional sales opportunity (perhaps I can sell to my old contact at his or her new location) the first five questions telegraph our abject terror when we realize how dependent we are on a single person to keep a major account. And—if you have had the account over ninety days—it is your own fault if you are in this mess.

Our customers—new and old, good, bad, and indifferent—are always at risk. Some experts estimate that today's graduates will have three or four separate careers in their lifetimes, not to mention separate jobs and job titles. Buyers change positions all the time. It's our job to build a web of relationships with every customer we serve—a web that will help us keep the business if (*when!*) our key contact decides to move on to other job opportunities.

Here's an example. Suppose you sell raw materials to a manufacturing plant. You first won the business with an open bid, but you have been able to keep it for the past eighteen months without rebidding. You even slid in a price increase about eight months ago. You feel like you are giving the company good service, but in the eighteen months you have dealt with this company you have never interacted with anyone but the purchasing manager.

Right out of the gate, you have made a bad mistake. After eighteen months you should be webbed so tightly to this account that it would take a buzz saw to cut you loose. You haven't done that, and all your sales volume with this account is clearly at risk. It's your own fault, bubba.

That said, let's think about the other people (and job titles) with whom you could build a relationship to "web" yourself to this account. After eighteen months you should, at a minimum, have relationships with three of the following, and the relationship should focus on some or all of the areas identified:

1. **The Engineering Department**—Is the product arriving as specified? Can you help the engineers respec the product so they can get a better result? Can you help them respec it so your company is the only supplier who can bid to supply the product? *How can you help them save money?*
2. **The Plant Manager**—What problems is he or she having related to producing the products that use your raw materials? *What information do you have that would help solve these problems?*
3. **The Quality Control Department**—Any issues here? *What do they need from you?*
4. **End Users/Operators on the Plant Floor**—*What ideas do these folks have that could help you help them?* Is there a raw material they like better than yours? Why do they like it better? Can you win them over? If so how?
5. **Accounts Payable**—Are your invoices appropriate and easy to read? Do the Payables folks need something on the invoices they are not getting? *How can*

you be helpful to them?

6. **The Receiving Department**—Is your material arriving in a way that is easy for them to handle? Is it palletized in ways that they can store it with few hassles? *How can you help them?*

Look again at the queries that follow each of the department listings above. In *each* case you are saying—sometimes overtly, sometimes more subtly—"What are your problems, and how can I help you solve them?" This is the same question we began with in Steps 2 and 3 of the sales process —it is the question that undergirds all sales relationships. People buy to solve a problem, and people keep buying from you only as long as you continue to solve their problems better than any of your competitors.

The great advantage of building a relationship web with your customers is two-fold:

1. The web protects you from having only one point-of-contact with your accounts, and
2. The web gives you many more sources of data as you seek to understand and solve the problems this customer faces vis-à-vis your product.

Build that relationship web—it's good for you *and* for the customer.

Making Common Courtesy a Competitive Edge

I once heard a speaker lament, "Common sense ain't near as common as it used to be!" He was right, of course, as you have no doubt observed. An appropriate corollary might be:

> *"Common courtesy ain't near as common as it used to be, either!"*

Thank people for their business. You'd be surprised how far that will go. And it needn't be an extravagant thanks either—the effectiveness of a thank-you seems to have a more direct tie to the sincerity of the thanks than to the dollars spent on the gesture.

Here's an example—brief but powerful. I have an acquaintance who used to be CEO and chairman of one of the southeast's largest banks. It was a big damn job, and this guy had a lot on his plate. An executive at a small graphic design firm—a minor supplier to this mega-bank—got promoted, and my friend took time to write a brief, personal, handwritten, congratulatory note. He never heard a word of thanks. And he never forgot it, either.

When people put themselves out for you, they deserve to be acknowledged and thanked. Beyond that, many folks *expect* to be thanked. We ignore those expectations at our great peril. Pick up your pen and write that note. Pick your phone and make that call. Thank people when they help you—and buying your product certainly qualifies as "helping you out."

Remember: "Common courtesy ain't near as common as it used to be!" Relate to your customers from a position of gratitude and you will make manners a point of competitive advantage for you and your products.

Planning and Goal Setting—A Key to a Successful Life in Sales

"If you fail to plan, then plan to fail!" My first sales manager said this to me years and years ago. I believed him then because he was the boss. I now know—through my own long experience and keen observation—that he was telling the truth.

There is a story, perhaps apocryphal, about the champion golfer Gary Player. Player was famous for many things—he always wore black, he won many championships, and he practiced *a lot*. He was once asked about a championship he won, and the reporter made an offhand comment about Player being lucky. Player responded, "You know, it's funny. The harder I practice, the luckier I get!"

The same can be said of planning: the more thoroughly you plan, the luckier you will get. Few things worth achieving in life just *happen*. Set specific goals and work for them—measuring your progress as you go.

The people around you can help you with your goal-setting more than I can in a book of this type, because the particulars of sales goal setting are often unique to each business. Even so, here are several pointers that may be useful. As you set goals, make sure your targets are *SMART*. That is, make sure every sales goal you set satisfies each of the criteria below. Your goals must be:

***S**pecific*—your goals need to specify exactly what you are going to achieve. *How much volume* are you going to do? In *which products*? At *what price points* and *what margin*? From *which customers* and *market segments*? *Be clear with about specific goals*, or you will not be able to tell if you ever reached them!

***M**easurable*—how are you going to measure progress towards the goal? What's the yardstick? When do you measure? Who keeps score?

***A**ttainable*—the goal needs to be tough enough to make you stretch, but not so hard that you give up in frustration and quit.

***R**elated*—relate your goals to things that matter to you. How will you benefit if you reach your goal? How will your team or workgroup benefit? How will the customer benefit? How will the company benefit?

Time-based—when is the due date? Most work gets done the day before it's due—set a due date to make yourself work, and so you will know when to keep score.

Once you have learned to frame clear goals, you still have to do your planning. Most large companies force the sales organization to plan annually as part of the budgeting process, and that's a good place to start. But successful selling requires a series of plans, many of which have to be updated far more often than annually. Among the plans you might need to develop—depending on the product or service you are taking to market—are:

- An account plan—how are you going to maximize satisfaction in—and revenue from—each account?
- A prospect plan—how are you going to develop new accounts to grow your territory and supplement those accounts that are losing market share and sales volume?
- A territory development plan—how are you going to generate the most revenue and profit from a particular sales territory?
- A career development plan—how are you going to manage your career and sell yourself (the *only* product you are *always* stuck with) to your management for promotion? If you are worn out with your management, how are you going to leverage your successes in this job to get your next job? How do you prove you are good at the skills that feed your family?

Without falling too deeply into stereotype, planning and goal-setting are skills that the typical salesperson often lacks. I once heard a sales manager say of an employee, "He goes out, gets in his car, and heads off in whatever direction the car is pointed. And that's the extent of his planning."

At the beginning of a career, lack of planning is not an insurmountable obstacle. Hard work, determination, and will-to-win can—and often *do*—overcome lots of shortcomings. Interestingly, it is will-to-win that most often moves salespeople to develop planning skills. You cannot get to the highest levels of sales or sales management without the ability to craft and execute a detailed sales plan. And a detailed sales plan is comprised of dozens of discrete, tightly defined, *SMART* sales and performance goals.

So attack your sales planning with vigor and tenacity: succeed to plan while you plan for success.

Managing the Sales Process—The Tickler File and Other Tools

I am the worst possible person in the world to tell you how to manage paper and contacts with your customers—not because I am bad at it, I'm not. But I have no system—I seem to intuitively know and remember when it is time to call a customer. I have a sixth sense, if you will, for how to maintain these key relationships.

It works for me, but I wouldn't recommend it. For one thing, it is impossible to explain to your manager—and it will alternately scare the heck out of him and drive him nuts.

Who wants to make their manager nuts when it is so easy to avoid? Further, this intuitive, I-just-know-in-my-gut-system is impossible to teach to a new salesperson. (I know, I've tried!) So when you move into sales management you will find yourself saying, "Don't do as I do, do as I say!" And that's not a good recipe for human relationships *or* for management.

Let me just say this: there are dozens of tools out there that can make managing your customers, your contacts, and your follow-ups far easier than you ever hoped or imagined. There is contact management software that will give you prompts for all the key information you need to track a prospect. There are tickler files and suspense files and all manner of tools that can keep you on track and out of the ditch. My best advice for finding and selecting these tools is twofold. As a first step, ask your manager—and the best-organized salesperson you know—how each of them manages their contacts and follow-up. See if the system they use might work for you. As a second step, go to a good office supply store and ask someone for counsel in selecting some tools. Contact and follow-up management is an intensely personal discipline, and you need to find the tools that will work best for you, your circumstances, and your sales style.

I have told you where the landmine is: if you don't manage the customers you can never make them customers for life. I can't teach you how to do it, because my system is not one that will likely work for you. So find someone who can teach you how to use these tools, and learn from them whatever you need to learn to do a good job following-up for yourself and your customers.

Following-Up for an Ongoing, Profitable Relationship

One of the greatest lessons I ever learned in selling came from a mentor who was also a Presbyterian minister. He had discovered that the best way for him to serve the world was by consulting in business and industry. For a while I worked alongside him on a number of projects. His constant question to me during the time we worked together was this:

> *"What are you going to sell them next?"*

The question used to drive me bonkers—he'd ask it the minute you walked in the door from the initial sale. You hadn't even had thirty seconds to savor the first sale, and he wanted to know what the *next* sale will be! Give it a rest, will you?

But he was right. It's always important—and especially in professional services—to be on the lookout for the next thing you are going to sell a client. And this is not merely self-serving pocket-lining either.

Remember, customers buy to solve problems. No problem = no sale. On the other hand, most businesses (and hence most customers) have many, many problems. Just because you have made one sale and solved one problem does not mean that you have done all you can to serve the customer with whom you are interacting. So we need to always be scanning the horizon for other sales opportunities, other problems to solve, other ways we can make life easier for the customer by taking him or her out of the hassle business.

The key questions we ask are:

- What other problems can I solve for this customer? *and*
- What else can I sell this customer?

And we do the customer no service by letting an apparent problem go unacknowledged and unsolved when we are working with them.

An example: suppose for a moment that you are an accountant. You have been pursuing a local business for several months and they finally contact you. They want you to assemble data they provide and then compile a Profit and Loss Statement, a Balance Sheet, and a Sources and Uses Schedule. You dutifully do your tasks, then submit the work and the invoice. Job done! Bill paid! Sale made!

But have you really done this client justice?

Perhaps not. Because in compiling the statements it seemed to you that the client was overpaying taxes by a tremendous amount. You talked briefly to the bookkeeper, but he seemed defensive and resistant to giving you much information—perhaps he saw you as a threat. Do you just drop the issue?

No! Don't *drop* the issue; *raise* the issue! The customer has an apparently-real problem—he is overpaying taxes by a significant amount. Surely he would welcome the chance to have you audit his records, and identify ways he could pay less in taxes than he is currently paying. He wins. And you have figured out what to sell him next...

Always be on the lookout for what you are going to sell them next. Let your guide be this question: *What other problems does this client have that I can help him or her solve?*

Pay Attention to Customer Complaints

When I work with salespeople who are trying to repair ruptured relationships with their customers I hear one refrain over and over again: "They don't take me seriously when I complain; they blow off my concerns."

And that's too bad. Because ignoring customer feedback is the very best way to lose a customer. Interestingly, customers often make an initial purchase from a new supplier using criteria that are somewhat different from the criteria that this same customer will use to evaluate an ongoing supplier. The differences can be summed up easily in two brief sentences:

> *Price, quality, and functionality get you in.*
> *Response time, service, and support get you out.*

Prospects decide to give us a try based on the quality of our product, how well they think it will work (functionality), and how much we are charging for it. Once onboard as a customer, our accounts *assume we will continue to deliver these three things* (price, quality, and functionality). And these three things alone are not enough. They got us into the arena, but they will not—by themselves—keep us in the game.

To keep the customers we have worked so hard to garner, we also have to provide the response time, service, and support that make us easy to do business with. Once you get a customer, it's not an either/or equation. It's not price *or* service. It's not quality *or* support. Once you get a customer, it's a both/and deal: both 1) price, quality, functionality *and* 2) response time, service, and support.

Listen to your customers. The will tell you their problems. They will tell you how to sell them. And they will tell you how to keep them happy.

A Successful Customer Relationship Is a Marriage, Not a Date

As you live with your customers, you will realize that a successful customer relationship is more like a good marriage than a hot date. Sure, there's the ecstasy of the first sale, and the rush of excitement when you begin to work together. But neither of these lasts forever, and you begin to see the weaknesses and inherent craziness of your customer—just as they begin to see the same in you. They have bad days; you have bad days. Don't give in.

The sales relationships that work best (and I've been using the same print shop for twenty years, so I know) are those where each side values the other, and takes the long view of the relationship. You don't have to make money on every transaction, just like they don't have to get the absolute lowest price every time. You are in it for the long haul. Value each other and treat each other with respect.

And—like my great aunt told me one time regarding relationships—"Don't let the sun go down on your anger if you can help it."

A successful customer relationship is like a *marriage*, not like a *date*. Value your customers. Forgive them their foibles. Celebrate your mutual successes. And don't forget to say "Thank you!"

Getting Down to Cases: Making It Real in Your Work Life

This stuff only works if you do—if you take it out of this book and put it into play in the sales that feed your family and keep you employed. Reflect back on the material in chapter 11, and then answer the questions below.

1. How do you feel about follow-up? Is it relatively easy for you, or do you prefer the hunt and the kill to the details of cleaning and field-dressing your prey?

   ____

   ____

   ____

2. How would you behave differently if you treated follow-up as the first step in the next sale, rather than as the last, hassle-filled step of the previous sale?

3. Have you ever had problems because the people in your organization did not value your customers as much as you value them? Name a couple of specific accounts where this has been a problem. What happened?

4. How can you "sell" your new accounts to internal folks so that they will value the accounts as much as you value them? List five accounts where you need to sell your customer to your internal customer-care people. When will you begin this process?

5. List below your five most important customers. How many contacts do you have at each of these customers? What is your plan to build a "web" of relationships within each account, so your position in the account is less vulnerable? ________________________

____

____

____

____

____

6. Do you regularly take time to thank your customers for doing business with you? How can you make courtesy a point of competitive advantage in relating to your customers? ________________________

____

____

____

7. "If you fail to plan, then plan to fail." Do you find this to be true? How do you use planning to make sure you solve your customers' problems and achieve your business goals? ________________________

____

____

____

8. "Price, quality, and functionality get you in. Response time, service, and support get you out." Think back on the two biggest accounts you have lost in your selling career. Be sure to tell yourself the whole truth about these account losses. What were the biggest factors in losing these accounts? Did the lost accounts bear out the aphorism above? Why did you answer as you did?

____

____

____

____

____

Key Reminders

- Follow-up is one of the hardest parts of the entire selling process.
- Follow-up—like the initial sale—is all about solving customer problems.
- Follow-up sales can be the most profitable sales for you and for your company.
- Follow-up represents the beginning step for the next sale to this customer or company.
- A satisfied customer can be an excellent source of referrals.
- Keep Your Commitments!—This is the Cardinal Rule of selling.
- Write it down!—Who is going to do what for whom by when using what resources and for what compensation?
- Price, quality, and functionality get you in. Response time, service, and customer support get you out.

12
Launching Your Sales Ship for a Successful Voyage

As a small boy I was occasionally given plastic models of airplanes and ships as birthday gifts. Given my proclivity for action over reflection, I would always plunge right in—assembling the models without the slightest glance at the instructions. I usually got a pretty good outcome—"when in doubt, attack" is not the worst philosophy for someone headed for a career in sales. But I was inevitably left with a pile of miscellaneous parts at the end of the project—parts that were no doubt important, but didn't seem to fit anywhere on the model.

Likewise, you've reached the "miscellaneous parts" of our time together—important topics that we need to address, but that don't fit neatly into the sales process or any of the other chapters we have reviewed. We'll begin with rejection and discouragement—intrinsic components of life in sales. Then we'll move to "winging it"—a common temptation. And we'll look at a host of other issues, too—all of them issues we must deal with if we are to survive and thrive in the rough and tumble of selling.

Rejection—The Hardest Part of the Selling Game

Rejection is the most painful part of the selling game. There—I've said it. And I waited this long to say it because it's not news to you. I wanted to give you lots of tools to raise your closing ratio and minimize the number of times you hear "no" before I talked about this cruelest part of selling.

No matter the number of tools you have, though, "no" is a fact of life in the world of sales. Think about it this way: if every customer talks to at least four salespeople before making a single purchase, 75 percent of the salespeople will ultimately hear a "no." Just today I got a call with an estimate to paint my house—I now have seven estimates. Six of those people—over 85 percent—are going to hear "no". It's a fact of life in the selling business. So what can we do?

The first thing you can do is to get as good as you can at the job that feeds your family. Learn all the steps of the sales process, and learn how to recognize where you are as you move through the steps. Learn the features of your product, program, or service up one side and down the other—then *only talk about the features that matter to your prospective customer*. Bridge from your features to the benefits that solve the customer's problem, ask for the order, then circle back to probe and question when you get objections. All of this will help, *and* you're still going to get a lot of turn-downs. What to do? I have four suggestions:

1. Don't take the rejection personally.

The hell of selling is that the people who do sales best are the ones who can and do *personalize* it. They are the ones who connect with their customers on more than a business level, the ones who bring all that they have and all that they are to the selling situation. (See "Personalizing the Sale—Selling from the Core of Who You Are" in the paragraphs that follow.) It is hard for folks like this (I know, I am one of them) not to take rejection personally. Still, it's important counsel, because *the rejection is not likely about you.*

Think about all the possible criteria that a customer has when walking into a purchase. Where do you think the personality of the salesperson ranks? Not very high, I'd guess. Surely, it's way behind quality, the capacity of a product to solve the problem, price, service, timing, and a host of other buying criteria. It would be a sloppy buyer who would buy any high-value product based primarily on the salesperson's personality.

So they are not rejecting *you*—they are rejecting *your business proposition.* And you can learn from that experience, if you ask the right questions.

2. Learn what you can from every rejection.

Ironically, once you have learned that you did not get the business, it's often easier to get in for a follow-up visit with the buyer. He or she has made the decision, so the heat's off of you both. So take 'em to lunch and see what you can learn. (It's a great place to practice the questioning and listening skills from the Discovery Step—Step 3—in our sales process.)

As you listen to the buyer, invite him or her into your confidence and try to uncover exactly why the sale went to someone else. And never take the first answer you get at face value—probe gently until you *get to the root cause of the buyer's decision.* Most often you will find that there were multiple reasons why you lost the sale, none of which had anything to do with a major character flaw on your part.

Remember as you meet with the prospective customer that he or she is currently in Quadrant 2 of the Problem-Awareness Grid we reviewed in chapter 8. (They don't have a problem—since they just solved it by buying from someone else—and they know they don't have a problem.) The proper sales response in Quadrant 2 is "build the relationship and wait." And *meeting with them is part of building the relationship*—inviting them into your training, and getting them to coach you on how to be a better salesperson.

If you find that you lost the sale due to things beyond your control (price, product specs, credit terms, delivery timing, etc.) take the information back to the folks in your company who can make the changes that will give you a better shot at the sale next time. And *tell the prospect* that you are going to take this information back—that his or her feedback will help make your company better, and that next time you will be more competitive when it comes time to select a vendor. He'll appreciate being taken seriously, and your relationship will deepen.

3. Play the percentages.

I once worked with a fellow named Charlie Johnson—one of the half-dozen best salespeople I have ever met. He told me once that his closing ratio was about one in ten calls. So every time he got a no he said to himself, "I'm ten percent of the way to a yes!"

I like Charlie's thinking here! Selling requires, of course, 100 percent effort on *every* call; you can't just lay down after nine refusals, assuming that the tenth call is an automatic yes. But it does help reframe the no from pure rejection to one more step on the way to an eventual yes. Which—if you work the sales process—it doubtless is.

One caveat: as you track your own performance numbers, pay special attention to the percent of calls that actually result in a sale. This number (called the *closing ratio*, as in the above example) can give you insight into how well you are doing over time. If the number begins to drop, something is wrong. Your prospect flow may be of poorer quality, external economic factors may be amiss, or you may need to brush-up on your selling skills. All things being equal, your closing ratio should go up over time as you become more adept at selling.

4. Remember: they can't hate you; they don't even know you!

My wife is a first-class business and corporate trainer; she does lots of work in the area of presentation skills and stand-up training. I have heard her give this admonition to many of her classes:

> *"Whenever you stand up in front of a group, the group immediately breaks down into three clusters:*
>
> - 1/3 of them immediately love you—you remind them of a favorite teacher, someone they used to date, or they somehow just connect with you.
> - 1/3 of them instantly hate you—you remind them of someone who dumped them, of a mean teacher in elementary school, of someone they already dislike intensely.
> - 1/3 of them are open—they have not decided how they feel about you yet.
>
> *Whenever you make a presentation (or a sales call, for that matter) you are playing for that middle third. And the best you could ever do is wind up with 2/3's of the folks in your camp."*

Laura's counsel is well-taken. Your prospective customers don't even *know* you—how could they hate you?

Rejection of your sales proposal is not rejection of you. And even if it was—why would it matter? Your worth arises from far more than your performance as a salesperson.

Your worth is derived from your service to your community, your relationship to your friends and family, your own self-understanding, and your relationship to your religious tradition, and the Ground of Being that informs your life. None of these things changes when you lose a sale.

T. S. Eliot began his poem *The Waste Land* with the words "April is the cruelest month..." The poem speaks to the promise of new life in April, and how that new life is engendered—and can be cut short by—the vagaries of weather. *Selling* is similar to *April* in some regards—the promise of the sale and the excitement of the chase can be cut short by the whims of the buyer. It's not about you, generally. Don't take it personally.

Like nature—which recovers when the late frost kills the blooms on the citrus trees and cuts the crop in half, salespeople have to soldier-on in the fact of rejection. Take the rejection, learn what you can, and move on. You'll live to sell another day!

Discouragement—An Occupational Hazard of Selling

If rejection is a root cause, discouragement can be a result. Days and days of cold calls, writing letters, dialing and smiling, emails, and even door slams begin to take a toll. The time comes when we begin to feel like Willy Loman in

Arthur Miller's *Death of Salesman*—we are discouraged. We may even move past discouraged to old-fashioned despondent. What do we do?

This question is worth the asking. Even the best of hitters in baseball occasionally needs one-on-one coaching to get out of a batting slump. Even Tiger Woods has a coach to help him with his swing. Why shouldn't you and I have a sales coach? Why shouldn't we have someone to whom we can turn for advice and counsel when we seem to have lost our mojo? We *should* have a someone to whom we can turn. In fact, we should have *several* "someones" to whom we can turn. I suggest you assemble a team of people who can help you grow as a salesperson; your ideal team would include each of the following:

A Peer-Partner

This can be someone from your workplace or someone from outside your company who makes their living in sales. Peer-partners are especially useful for swapping tips, encouraging each other when things are difficult, and role-playing sales situations when developing new skills. Be alert in your peer-partner relationship. Don't start having so much fun with each other that you quit encouraging and supporting each other professionally and just sit around shooting the breeze and yucking it up.

Your Boss/Sales Manager

Your manager is not your best friend, your buddy, or a useful peer-partner. If anyone has ever told you that these are appropriate roles for you manager, let me burst your bubble now. Your manager is the person who can fire you—don't ever lose sight of that, or you two may disappoint each other.

That said, a manager can (and *should*, if he or she is doing the job the way it is supposed to be done) be a useful asset in helping you develop your skills as a professional salesperson. People get to be sales managers on two basic tracks:

1. They are either good at selling, or
2. They are good at administrative bullshit.

Either track is okay, but you need to know how your manager got his or her job so you will know what he or she can teach you.

If your manager was good at selling, she or he probably can't tell you how they did what they did. For most really good salespeople, selling is something they cannot articulate. But they can *do* it. Fair enough. Get them to make some calls with you—let them sell and you watch. Take good notes, then spend an hour or so after the call debriefing the details of what you saw. Ask them why they did *everything* they did. Be sure to get beyond *what* they did to *why* they did it, because that's where the real learning takes place.

Then reverse roles—you do the selling while your manager takes notes and observes. Debrief this session as intensely as you did the first one. You'll be amazed what you can learn. And this is the very best type of learning, too—you've got a one-on-one tutor!

Suppose your sales manager was an adequate salesperson—perhaps even a pretty good one—but you feel that you can already outsell him or her. Fair enough—that's more often true than you might know. In fact, I had a dear friend who worked for a company that actually gave salespeople a choice—they could move into sales management, or they could stay on the sales track for their entire career—with no cap on earnings and no penalty for not moving into management. My friend stayed in sales, and eventually wound up being managed by someone younger, lower paid, and less adept at selling than she was. It worked out fine. The manager knew things other than one-on-one selling; he was good at running institutional interference for my friend, who hated that kind of stuff.

If your manager is a middling salesperson but is a crackerjack administrator, the fates have smiled down on you! Get him or her to teach you all they know; it will be invaluable for the rest of your career. We've already seen (chapter 11, sales Step 8) how critical follow-up is to maximize revenue and profitability from an account. A crack administrator can teach you lessons about this that you could never learn on your own initiative. (And can also likely keep you from stepping on administrative landmines that could blow off your entire lower body.)

Crack administrative sales managers can also help you figure out how to network your clients/accounts/customers into the entire company, so that a web of people in your organization supports the account, not you alone.

Use your manager—that's why he or she is there. Make them teach you what they know. It'll put you a leg up in your company, and way ahead of your deadwood peers who avoid the manager because he or she is "the boss." But always remember—he or she is boss first. Don't get confused about that. It can be painful—*very* painful. I know.

A Mentor-Coach

Why do I need a coach, you ask? I've got the boss. I've got a peer partner. Who needs a coach, on top of all that? You do—unless you are Zig Ziglar or Tom Hopkins!

Tiger Woods has got a coach. Lance Armstrong has a team of them. Barry Bonds has got one. Can you sell better than Tiger can play golf, or Lance can cycle, or Barry can hit? Point made.

So you need a coach—for what? You need someone outside the organization—someone who understands the ins and outs of selling—to whom you can tell the *whole* truth. Someone with whom you can talk about frustrations and challenges and irritations—and all this with no threat of repercussions. He can't fire you—you don't even work for him or her.

You also need—perhaps even more so—someone who will *tell you the whole truth*. Your peer-partner won't do it, because he has to live with you. He spends so much time with you that you co-opt each other; you start playing nice and dodging the hard questions of life and sales development. Your boss won't do it—unless you make him or her really mad—for the same reasons. He or she has to live with you. And if they really irritate you, you might quit on them, or go around them to *their* boss.

But your mentor-coach will tell you the truth. Because that's what you contracted for—it's what you expect from him or her, and what you likewise offer to him or her. And it's priceless.

Other Methods to Fight Discouragement

So build yourself a team of folks who can help you—a peer-partner, your sales manager, and a mentor-coach. Building your skills and having someone to talk with is the beginning of keeping discouragement at bay. There are other things you can do to stave off discouragement, however, and they are also important.

Find a way to de-stress.

Find something that takes pressure off of you, rather than adding to the pressure you experience day-to-day in your job. For many salespeople, this can be a hobby such as golf, tennis, or fishing. It doesn't matter so much what you choose, as that you *choose something*.

Once you have found the thing that gives you pleasure and de-stresses you, then discipline yourself to do that thing. If you choose golf, then *go play golf*—don't just drive around with your sticks in the trunk and good intentions of going to play a few holes. If you choose fishing, you have to *go fishing*. Psychological fishing (thinking about fishing as you drive to your next call or fill out your call reports) does not count.

A final caution: beware that your career doesn't eat into your de-stressing activity. If you begin to make all your golf dates into sales opportunities, you have missed the point. Golf is a great way to be with customers. And golfing with customers does not count as de-stressing.

Build a life outside of work.

One reason that work (and sales in particular) can be so stressful and so discouraging is that we began to believe that our sales numbers define us. In a very real sense, these numbers do go a long way to defining us within the constraints of our jobs. But your job is not your entire life. And that is one reason you build a life outside of work.

Vocational counselors often speak of the struggles of people who have worked at a job for fifteen or twenty years and are suddenly laid off. For years these folks defined who they *are* by what they *do*. Now they no longer do that thing anymore, and they don't know who they are. They find themselves saying, "If who I am is what I do, who am I when I don't do that anymore?" And it can be a wrenching question…

So build a life outside of work. Cultivate friendships. Be a wonderful spouse and parent and child and sibling. These people all know you as something other than a unit of production. They value you for who you are, and not just for your performance versus quota in the last quarter. And all of that can serve as a powerful salve when the sales world wounds you with repeated messages that say you are not good enough.

Give yourself away.

It is interesting how many of the world's great religious traditions hold up service as a one of humanity's highest callings. Most of us can name several people who changed our lives dramatically, even though they entered our lives in a strictly volunteer capacity: scout leaders, little league coaches, grade-parents in school, Red Cross volunteers.

Often the surest way to find one's self is to lose one's self in the service of others. And one of the surest ways to lose one's sense of discouragement is to find one's self in giving to others. So give yourself away—lead a Junior Achievement group, tutor at a preschool, volunteer as a coach for a local ball team. *You are more than your sales numbers*—and these pursuits will serve as a tangible reminder of all the ways in which you are more than your numbers.

Connect to something beyond yourself.

I'll be straight with you—I am talking about God here. I don't mean that you have to drag yourself to church or mosque or temple—though you might also find that very helpful. What I do mean is that life is short (and often hard—especially in some parts of the world) and then you die.

As someone in the world of sales, you will be more exposed than most people to notions of survival of the fittest. And you are apt to work for bosses who are more driven and less mentally healthy than the norm of polite society. If your feet are not standing on the solid rock of something beyond yourself, life is going to kick you in the teeth. (Life is going to kick you in the teeth anyhow, but it might be easier to take if you are grounded in a belief.

So find out what you believe about God. If you are comfortable in the religion of your youth, by all means stay in it. If you hated the faith of your fathers and mothers, explore something else. Go into this experience with your mind (and your heart) wide open—willing to savor whatever God might have available for you. This is important work—far beyond the importance of honing your skills as a salesperson.

I once worked as a chaplain at a major university medical center. It's axiomatic that—as someone is dying—they rarely look up and say, "You know, I wish I had spent more time at work..." What they *do* wish for is that they had more answers to the questions that really matter. And the questions they ask are ones like these: "Why am I here? Is there a God? If there is a God, is this God for me or against me? If there is a God, and God is for me, then how should I live?"

So ground your life in something beyond your sales performance. You are more than the sum of your quotas—even if you exceed them by a large margin!

Personalizing the Sale—Selling from the Core of Who You Are!

Here's a story; see what you think.

Some years ago I was working hard to cultivate a million dollar prospect in the automotive battery business. I was based in North Carolina; the potential customer was in San Antonio, Texas. I flew to San Antonio several times to understand the customer's problems (Discovery—Step 3) and to clearly articulate (Making the Case—Step 5) how our program attributes (those are the features) could solve his problems (those are the benefits). These guys still wouldn't get off the dime. They just couldn't decide (Objection—Step 6).

Finally, I had had enough. Plane tickets aren't cheap. Every sales call took two full days to make. I had asked for the business every way I knew how. What could I do? I was about out of tricks.

I had one last, desperate brainstorm. I sent a colleague to a local variety store and got half a dozen inexpensive men's weddings rings—big rings, because these were massive, Texas guys. I wrote each of them a letter, the gist of which went something like this:

You know, guys, we have been on several dates. You've eaten my steaks and you've drunk my liquor. I like you; you like me. We have a hell of a good time together. You've got a problem and I can solve it. I want to do business with you, and I'd like to start sooner rather than later. But I'm looking for a marriage, not a date.

If you want to make a long-term commitment to a supplier—one who will make a long-term commitment to you—then I'm your guy. If you're just looking for a date—if all you want to do is eat my steak and drink my liquor—I ain't coming back.

Here's my proposal: Let's get married and make each other a lot of money. I'll call you in the next three days to see what you think of my proposal.

Lots of love,
Frank McNair
Director of Sales and Marketing

You may think I'm crazy—and that puts you in darn good company, I'll tell you that. But this *worked.* The guys convulsed with laughter and took it all in good humor. I had called them on yanking me around (I was young and relatively new to the business; they were old veterans) and they knew it. We signed the deal less than three months later.

Could this work for you? I don't know, because I don't know *you.*

I *do* know that the more of your unique personality you can bring to a sale, the more you differentiate yourself from every other yahoo who is chasing the prospective customer. And the more you are differentiated, the more likely you are to make that sale. (Remembering, of course, that the prospective customer is the one who gets to decide if your antics are appropriate, on-target, or move the sale forward.)

Here's another story; see what you think.

Some years ago I was contemplating a job change. I targeted a number of companies, and had good luck getting interviews with all but one of my hit list. But I never got a response from the one company in which I was especially interested. How could I break through the clutter and wind up on the decision-maker's desk?

Finally—though it was only a thirty-mile drive from my office to his office—I FedExed my resume to the president of the company. My cover letter talked about my ability to act quickly while developing innovative solutions to knotty problems—including my problem of getting through to him personally. The president called me the day he got the FedEx envelope—we met before the week was out.

Should you start FedExing all your correspondence? Not necessarily. For one thing, this was a number of years ago—the novelty of a FedEx envelope has worn off substantially. Further, FedEx's competitors (including the United States Postal Service) have developed look-alike products that cost less and further dilute the impact of those brightly-colored, sturdy cardboard envelopes.

No—the point is not the proposal of marriage or the FedEx letter. The point is to stretch your brain and your approach so you can break out of the clutter and get noticed. To apply your unique spin to your work so that—at the end of the day—you stand out in a positive way.

As you give gifts or embrace gimmicks like the ones above, remember that gimmicks are most effective when they relate to the point you are trying to make. A coffee mug is nice, but if you don't sell mugs or coffee, it really doesn't *relate*.

My gimmicks—good, bad, or indifferent—related to the points I was trying to make. The wedding rings pointed to my desire to be in a long-term, committed relationship with my prospects—one where we worked on our problems together and did all we could to make the relationship grow and flourish. With the FedEx letter, I was trying to telegraph my willingness to do things differently in an attempt to get past formal screens and informal obstacles so I could get to my target audience.

Neither of these is brilliant—though I am pretty fond of the wedding ring idea—but both helped reinforce a point I was trying to make in my overall sales pitch.

You Can't Buff a Turd

You have looked at this headline and you have wondered, "What in the world is he talking about?" I know it's true, because that's how I felt the first time I heard that line.

Here's the story. I was once selling into a very competitive market. I had a superior product and not much else. My prices were high, my advertising allowances were low, and I had few other arrows in my sales quiver. I was grasping for ways to make the sale, and I began to speak glowingly of our support for the sell-through to the end customer. I spoke of how our sales force would help the distributor dramatically increase his market penetration and hence his sales volume. This entire conversation was taking place on the phone, and a deep silence ensued after I finished making my case. And then the customer replied: "Forget it, Frank. I've met your salespeople. You can't buff a turd. It just messes up the rag!"

My customer wasn't buying it—I couldn't put a happy face on something he saw as a major liability when I made the case for buying from my company.

So here's your takeaway: I do believe life is mostly packaging—that *how you say what you say matters just as much as what you say itself.* Even so, it's hard to put a happy face on some things. Some things you just can't package in a way they are palatable. So—when the customer has got you—concede the point he or she is trying to make, and move on. You may still be able to salvage the sale.

You can't buff a turd. It just messes up the rag!

A Closing Homily

Someone once asked me to summarize what this book was all about in less than two hundred words. I leave you with these words, along with my best wishes for much success in the world of sales.

So, I bet you thought you talked people into buying, huh? Not so. Think about it: has anyone ever talked you into anything that you are really glad you bought? Not likely. No, we don't talk our customers into buying—at least we don't if we ever want to sell to them again. Rather, we listen our customers into buying. We find out their needs and wants and problems, their hopes and dreams and aspirations. And then we tailor-make a solution—one that uses our product—to best meet their needs.

It's as simple (and as difficult) as that. I once heard it said this way, "Sell them every dollar of product and services they need, and not a penny more." And I couldn't agree more wholeheartedly. The customer is not the enemy. We are in this together. And—in the long view—we only win if they win.

Now go out and make those sales. With what you have learned in this book, I am more convinced than ever that you can make the sale!

That's All Folks!

As a child, my favorite cartoon shows signed off with a slide saying, "That's all folks!" And that *is* all. This is it—the end of the line—for you and me this time around. I'm convinced that—if you follow the process we've explored together—you *can* make the sale.

I'd love to hear about your successes, and what you learn along the way. Drop me a line at mcnairtraining@aol.com and let me hear from you.

Good luck and God bless.

Getting Down to Cases: Your Final Reflection on Takeaway

1. How do you deal with the rejection that is inherent in the world of selling? Of the four suggestions for dealing with rejection, which two were most familiar to you? Write them in the space provided. ___________
____
____

2. Of the four suggestions for dealing with rejection, which one do you need to embrace and use more often? Enter it below, then contract with yourself—select a start date for beginning to use this suggestion in your sales life. ______________________
____
____

3. How do you manage discouragement? Which of the suggestions are you going to weave into the tapestry of your sales life? When are you going to start? ______

______

______

4. Do you feel connected to something beyond yourself? Why did you answer as you did? Is this a part of your life you would like to develop more fully? How and when are you going to start? ______

______

______

5. What is your reaction to the two anecdotes about personalizing the sale? How have you personalized sales in the past? Has it worked? What else might you try?

______

______

______

6. Do you believe that *life is mostly packaging*—that how you say something matters almost as much as what you say? Why did you answer as you did? ______

______

______

7. Have you ever tried to *buff a turd*? Did you get caught? How did you extricate yourself from that jam? ______

____

____

8. What are the three key things you have learned in working with this book. What are you going to do—today—to put to use these three things you have learned? ______________________________

____

____

Key Reminders

- Rejection is the most painful part of the selling game.

- Four pointers for dealing with rejection:
  1. Don't take the rejection personally.
  2. Learn what you can from every rejection.
  3. Play the percentages.
  4. Remember: They can't *hate* you; they don't even *know* you!

- Rejection is a root cause, but discouragement can be a result.

- Four key ways to deal with discouragement:
  1. Find a way to de-stress.
  2. Build a life outside of work.
  3. Give yourself away.
  4. Connect to something beyond yourself.

- Personalize your sales for greater sales success

- Life is mostly packaging, but you can't buff a turd.

- Sell them every dollar of product and services they need but not a penny more.

- The customer is not the enemy. We are in this together. And we only win if they win.

- Three key sources of insight and advice when we seem to have lost our mojo can include our:
  1. Peer-Partners
  2. Boss/Sales Manager
  3. Mentors/Coaches

Index

A

adding value, 8
Alice in Wonderland question, 49

B

benefits, 146, 156, 163
  universal benefits, 147
bridging, 150, 152, 163

C

Campbell, David, 187
care about customers, 77, 86
Circular Sales Process, 260

closing, 234, 235, 236, 242, 243
  celebrate, 245
  dispel anxiety, 245
coach, 293, 294
cold calling, 90–92
combatant selling, 2
commitment, 260, 261, 277
common courtesy, 268–269
consumer behavior, 19
control, 11
credibility, 78

D

differential diagnosis, 101, 107
discouragement, 289

F

features, 139, 155, 156, 163
  intangible products, 142, 164
  parachute example, 141, 163
follow-up, 255–258, 274
framing questions, 129

G

Getting Down to Cases, 14, 33, 56, 71, 95, 131, 166, 200, 229, 250, 278, 304

H

hot buttons, 65, 67, 72

I

implied contract, 62
imposters, 191

J

Johnson, Charlie, 287

K

Key Reminders, 18, 37, 58, 74, 98, 136, 168, 202, 232, 253, 282, 307

L

landmines, 67, 70, 73
listen carefully, 101, 277

M

Making It Real, 16, 35, 72, 97, 133, 157, 159, 161, 230

O

objections, 206, 208, 209, 210, 228
  answer, 213
  buying signs, 224
  clarify, 212, 215
  phony objections, 217–219
  price, 220–221
  probing, 215, 222
  restate, 212
  turnover, 223

P

Path to Purchase, 26, 40, 59, 75, 79, 81, 90
clarify need, 29
develop purchase criteria, 30
exceptions to the path, 31
gather data, 28, 42
identify need/problem, 28, 44
identify options, 29
identify potential salespeople, 31
identify potential sources, 30
select preferred outlet and salesperson, 31
visit potential sources, 31
peer-partner, 290
personalize the sale, 298, 300
planning, 271, 272
Player, Gary, 269
price, 197–198
Problem-Awareness Grid, 172, 173, 185, 247
Quadrant 1, 174, 177, 178
Quadrant 2, 174, 178, 179, 180
Quadrant 3, 174, 180, 182
Quadrant 4, 175, 182, 183
problem-solving, 88

Q

question families, 121
question precisely, 101
question types, 111
  closed, 111–112
  open, 111–113
  probing 114–116
questioning pattern, 116
  funnel, 117
  hourglass, 119–120
  tepee, 118

R

rapport, 86, 88
real salespeople, 191
rejection, 284, 285, 289
relationship web, 264, 266, 267

S

sales managers, 291–293
Sales Process, 40, 51, 75, 81
  closing, 47, 233, 241
  dealing with resistance, 46, 205, 240

discovery, 44, 52, 103, 106, 108, 109, 239
features and benefits, 45, 137, 239
following-up, 48, 241, 255
meet and greet, 43, 54, 75, 82, 85, 238
presenting the solution, 45, 169, 240
research prior to the sale, 42, 60, 238
sample questions, 122
buying process, 125
competition, 124
core problem, 123
price, 124
product specs, 123
schmucks, 92
selling as service, 2, 3, 5, 9, 10, 237, 263
SMART, 270
solving customer problems, 19
image problems, 21
perceived problems, 23
real problems, 20

T

tie-down question, 194–196
trial close, 196, 226, 227
trust, 79, 84

About the Author

Frank McNair has been selling since the moment—a couple of hours after his birth—when he hollered his lungs out and got someone to change his diaper, bring him a bottle, and cover him with a warm blanket. In his early life he sold—among other things—lemonade, World's Finest Chocolate, magazine subscriptions, and books (door-to-door) for Southwestern Publishing Company.

Frank graduated from the University of North Carolina, where he was a Morehead Scholar. He also earned a graduate business degree from the Babcock Graduate School of Management at Wake Forest University.

His professional career includes a decade in sales and marketing management—including stints at the L'eggs Division of Sara Lee Corporation, and as Corporate Director of Sales and Marketing for an automotive parts manufacturer. Frank began his consulting practice in 1988. He has done sales training with a variety of clients and industries from coast-to-coast, including: Ferrari North America, Oakwood Homes Corporation, Amarr Garage Doors, Ellison (now Atrium) Windows and Doors, and

Krispy Kreme Doughnut Corporation.

Frank is also a sought-after personal coach and keynote speaker, in addition to his training and writing pursuits. With his wife, Laura, he conducts training in managerial and supervisory skills, sales, account management and negotiation, and presentations and effective public speaking.

Frank's first book—*It's OK to Ask 'Em to Work!*—was published in 2000 and has been translated into German, Spanish, and Arabic editions. Both that book and this one are available from your local bookstore or from any online bookseller. You can find out more about Frank's consulting practice, contact Frank, and order books at mcnairandmcnair.com. You can also visit www.howyoumakethesale.com for tips, training options, and other useful information.

In his life outside of work, Frank is a committed community volunteer. He is an associate member of an Episcopal Monastic Order for men, and earned a Certificate in Spiritual Formation from Columbia Theological Seminary.

Frank and Laura live with their beloved golden retriever, Gracie, in a house overlooking the woods in Winston-Salem, North Carolina.